Contemporary Piano Method
book 3

by Margaret Brandman

Exclusive distributors for Australia and New Zealand
Encore Music Distributors
227 Napier St, Fitzroy VIC 3065 Australia
Phone +61 3 9415 6677
Facsimile +61 3 9415 6655
Email sales@encoremusic.com.au

This book © Copyright 2018 by Margaret Brandman trading as Jazzem Music
46 Gerrale St, Cronulla NSW 2230 Australia
ISBN 978-0-949683-27-4
ORDER NUMBER MMP 8026
International copyright secured (APRA/AMCOS). All rights reserved.

Unauthorised reproduction of any part of this publication by any means,
including photocopying, is an infringement of copyright.

CONTEMPORARY PIANO METHOD - BOOK 3

INTRODUCTION

This method is designed to equip the student with the necessary skills to play both Classical and Modern music, including Popular and Jazz styles, with ease and understanding while giving experience in skills required for both classical and contemporary examination syllabi. The piano method is the central core of an integrated course which provides materials for ear-training (audio and workbooks), theory, technique, improvisation and repertoire pieces in all styles.

The methodology incorporates various learning styles or modalities, including:

* aural training
* spatial reasoning -visual, aural and tactile
* colour - to impart the meanings of the durations of the notes
* visualisation and the use of pictorial representations of the intervals
* the gestalt approach to topics (the whole view)
* knowledge of keyboard geography
* shape and pattern reading
* harmonic analysis
* improvisation
* transposition

Following on from book 2B in the series, Book 3 continues to feature:

The streamlined interval approach to reading.
This is achieved when the aural, tactile and visual aspects of music are combined so that students are able to read and play by following the flow of intervals. Level Three continues the development of *music speed-reading and learning skills* to a high degree by applying the skill to reading in C Clef.

Transposition
By combining the interval reading approach with *scale pattern thinking*, students are able to transpose music to other keys with ease. The added benefit of this skill is the security that is instilled in the performer for reading music in the written position in the more advanced keys.

Rhythm
This book expands students horizons by exploring less usual time signatures.

Keyboard Geography
The *keyboard pattern approach* is used to teach major, minor and modal scales. Students are required to close eyes and visualise their hands on the keyboard pattern for the key, before playing the scale and reading the music. Refer to the supporting publication *Pictorial Patterns for Keyboard Scales and Chords* for all these patterns.

Understanding Harmonic Structure and Modulation
A unique feature of this course is that it requires students to be actively engaged in the task of discovering the underlying harmonic structure of music, using the information to speed up the learning process, build an aural awareness of keys and chords, and to use as a basis for improvisation.

Adding to the knowledge of all scale tone triads and 7ths in major and minor keys and common chromatic triads covered in Level Two of this series, Book 3 explores the four-note Chromatic chords used in Classical Harmony, as well as altered 7th chords and the extension chords of the 9th, 11th and 13th. The modulation spider template found on page 20 is extended to include the standard chromatic chords used in Classical music. It can be photocopied and used to discover the modulations and family of chords for each new key. For the Advanced Spider for pieces in Minor keys, refer to Book 2B.

Keyboard Harmony and Improvisation
The knowledge of the sounds of various scales and chords and modes and their keyboard patterns is fostered so that they may be used as tools for improvisation. In this book the topic of *Root Progressions* is introduced. Students are shown how arrange pieces by supplying substitute chords to a progression. The book also continues to develop students' ability to play from printed chord symbols as well as being able to realize a figured bass.

Styles of Music
This book features a range of styles of music from polyphonic pieces and modal pieces to Swing Jazz, giving the styles and experience required to become both a professional musician in the popular field, and a competent and informed performer of classical and contemporary music. Parallels are drawn between the harmonic devices of the classical and modern composers.

To fully understand the theoretical concepts in this book, students are advised to work through the accompanying theory and aural texts and audio which are listed below.

I trust that the student will enjoy working through the method and will gain an appreciation of the variety of music and also the inter-relationship between music of different ages, countries and periods. It is my belief, as demonstrated with my own students over many years, that through the understanding of the workings of each piece, the study process is made easier and more interesting, the appreciation of sounds increases and the resulting performance of each piece is more meaningful to both performer and listener.

For more detailed information on the ideas and information in the series refer to my web site:

www.margaretbrandman.com

Margaret Brandman (Dr)
Ph.D (Mus/Arts), B.Mus.(Comp), T.Mus.A
F.Comp. ASMC., F.Mus.Ed.ASMC., L.Perf. ASMC
Hon.FNMSM., A.Mus.A., ASA T.Dip

INTEGRATED SUPPORT MATERIALS FOR THIS LEVEL
- Pictorial Patterns for Keyboard Scales and Chords
- Its Easy to Improvise
- Dreamweaving
- Twelve Timely Pieces
- Contemporary Modal Pieces
- Blues and Boogie-Woogie
- Six Contemporary Pieces
- Reflections - concert work for piano
- Sonorities - concert work for piano
- Static Ripples - Piano Duet

THEORY/AURAL
- Contemporary Aural Course - Sets 4 to 6
- Contemporary Aural Course - Set 7 Hear Your Chords!
- Contemporary Aural Course - Set 8 Hear More Chords!
- Contemporary Theory Workbook 2
- Contemporary Chord Workbooks 1 and 2
- Harmony Comes Together Book 1

CONTEMPORARY PIANO METHOD
BOOK THREE
CONTENTS

Reading Music in C Clef	6
No. 1 Hot Tamales, Brandman. Chromatic chord practice	8
Triad Arpeggios. Root Position	9
The Harmonic Series	10
No. 2 Swing Low Sweet Chariot. The Pentatonic Scale	11
No. 3 Bells of Buddha, Brandman.	12
More on the Harmonic Series. The Harmonic Series Scale	13
Realization of a Figured Bass	
Figured Bass Exercises. Section One – Root Position	14
Chromatic Chords	16
Chord Analysis by Degree Numbers	18
No. 4 Prelude by F. Chopin. Op. 28. No. 20	19
Advanced Modulation Spider template: Major Keys	20
CANON	
No. 5 Around Seven, Brandman.	21
Triad Arpeggios in Inversions	22
No. 6 Flying High. (Arpeggio study), Brandman.	24
Altered Dominant Seventh Chords	26
No. 7 Travellin' Song, Brandman.	28
Altered Major Seventh and Minor Seventh Chords	29
Figured Bass Exercises. Section Two – First Inversions	30
ROOT PROGRESSIONS **Step One** Cycle Progressions	32
No. 8 Allegro by J. Haydn, arranged for C Clef	36
INVENTION	37
No. 9 Invention No. XII by J. S. Bach	38

Figured Bass Exercises. Section Three – Second Inversion 40

Simple and Compound Interval Review 41

Extended chords (1) Ninths 42

ROOT PROGRESSIONS **Step Two** Substitute Chords (bII) 44

No. 10 Evanescence, Brandman. 47

No. 11 Le Petit Rien by F. Couperin, arranged for C Clef 50

Extended Chords (2) Elevenths 51

ROOT PROGRESSIONS **Step Three** Substitute Chords (vii dim) 52

The Modal Seventh Substitute Chord 54

No. 12 Invention No. XIII by J. S. Bach 55

Applying Root Progressions Steps, 1, 2 and 3

    No. 13 Seasons of Love, Brandman. 58

Four-Note Arpeggio Fingerings 61

Rondo Form and Sonata Form 62

No. 14 Mandala Song, Brandman. 63

Extended Chords (3) Thirteenths 66

No. 15 Polonaise by J. S. Bach, arranged for C Clef 67

No. 16 Shenandoah (Traditional) arranged by M. S. Brandman 68

Figured Bass Exercises. Section Four – Seventh Chords 72

The Development of Modes

    (1) Early Greek Modes 73

    (2) Early Church Modes and Plainchant 74

    (3) Notation 75

    (4) Modes in the Renaissance Period 77

    (5) Musica Ficta alterations and Systems of Tuning 77

No. 17 Tell Mee Daphne by G. Farnaby 78

    (6) Modern Use of the Modes 80

No. 18 The Ring-tail 'Possum, Brandman. 81

Improvisation and the Modes 82

Extension Notes 84

READING MUSIC IN C CLEF

There are three Clefs found in common use in music of today. They are the Treble or G Clef, the Bass or F Clef and the C Clef which can be used as either a Soprano, Mezzo Soprano, Alto, Tenor or Baritone Clef depending on where it is placed on the staff.

The C Clef was used to avoid the use of leger lines. The Alto, Tenor and Soprano clefs are still in use today while the Mezzo Soprano and Baritone clefs were in common use before 1750.

The Alto Clef is used by the following instruments of the orchestra: Viola and the older instruments the Viola d'Amore and the Viola da Gamba. Alto Trombone in Eb (Alto or Bass Clef).

The Tenor Clef is used by these orchestral instruments: Bassoon (Bass and Tenor Clefs), Tenor Trombone (Tenor and Bass Clef), Valve Trombone in Bb (Tenor or Bass Clef), Cello (Bass, Tenor or Treble Clefs), Double Bass (Tenor and Bass Clef).

The Soprano Clef is sometimes seen in Vocal Music up to the time of Brahms (1833–1897) while the Alto Clef was used for the Alto Voice and the Tenor Clef for the Tenor voice.

The Clef (French for 'key') is simply a device to enable the player to find his/her starting point. Piano music only uses the Bass and Treble Clefs. However it is very useful for a pianist to be able to read in C Clef.

Reading in all Clefs should be approached from the point of view of intervals. Those students who have been following this series of books through from the start, need only find the starting position and read in the usual manner from there on.

Those students who have not read by intervals before this point, are advised to refer to books 1 and 2 in this series to acquire this skill.

Reading in the C Clef will enhance your ability to transpose and will also give you the skills required to play orchestral scores in which instruments are playing in transposed keys and C Clefs as well as in Treble and Bass Clef.

If the exercises and pieces presented are written on the white notes only, apply the Hand-Position approach to sum up which fingerings will be needed for each section of music. If a key signature is indicated make sure that you follow the 'PATHWAY' of the scale concerned.

Play all exercises separate hands.

No. 1 Soprano Clef

No. 2 Mezzo Soprano Clef

No. 3 Alto Clef

No. 4 Tenor Clef

No. 5 Baritone Clef

Prior to playing this piece, establish the keyboard pattern or Pathway, for the key. Set the fingers along the pathway to start, then continue thinking in intervals along this path, for the remainder of the piece.

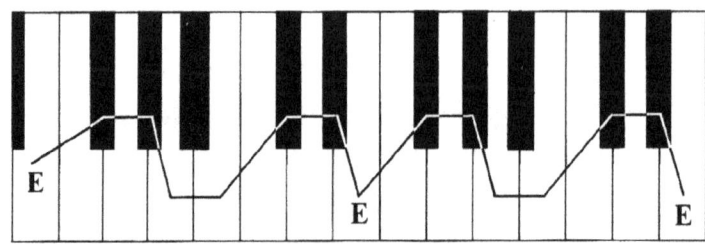

1. HOT TAMALES

Margaret S. Brandman

CHROMATIC CHORD PRACTICE

As well as practicing chords around the Cycle of Fifths it is wise to practise them moving up and down the notes of the Chromatic Scale.

Take C Major Triad in Root Position and move up the Chromatic scale to D♭ Major, D Major, E♭ Major chords and so on.

Then do the same with the First and Second Inversion of the triad. Taking a different one each day, practice all the Triads (Maj, Min, Dim, Aug, and Sus 4) and all the four-note chords you know in the same way.

ARPEGGIOS

An Arpeggio is a chord played in single notes successively over two or more octaves. To find the fingering for any arpeggio, take the first white note on the way up for the Right Hand and place the thumb on it. Then stretch the fifth finger to the octave above. Likewise, for the Left Hand find the first white note on the way down and place the thumb on it with the fifth finger an octave below.

Now, find the comfortable fingers for the required notes in between. For those Arpeggios starting on a white note this is an extremely easy process. You will find that the Right Hand fingering for all the Arpeggios beginning on White notes (Root Position) is: 123 1235 (over two octaves). The Left Hand fingering is 5421421, (over two octaves) for F, C and G Major triads and F, C, G, D, A, E and B Minor triads. For those Major triads with a black note as the third degree (D, A, E & B Majors) use 5321321.

Make sure that the thumb passes smoothly underneath the other fingers and that a good legato (smooth playing) is maintained throughout the Arpeggio. Angle the arms slightly, with elbows away from the body for better control.

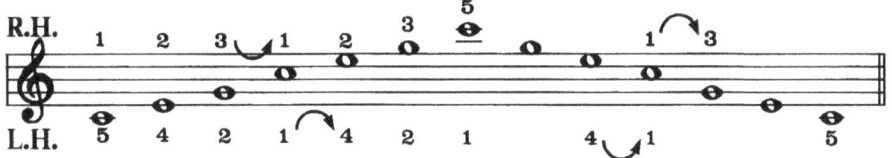

L.H. Same fingering for: Majors F, C, G; Minors F, C, G, D, A, E, B.

L.H. Same fingering for Majors: D, A, E, B.

ARPEGGIOS STARTING ON BLACK NOTES
(Root Position Only)

Firstly, there are two triads that have Black notes only. They are F Sharp Major chord and E♭ minor chord. The fingering of these two arpeggios is exactly the same as for those arpeggios with all white notes. The Right Hand fingering for both arpeggios is: 1 2 3 1 2 3 5. The Left Hand fingering for F sharp Major is: 5 3 2 1 3 2 1 (same as that for D Major) and the fingering for E♭ minor is: 5 4 2 1 4 2 1 (same as for E minor).

Secondly, the other arpeggios that **start** on a **black** note fall into two fingering groups. (1) All those that start on a black note except B♭. (2) B♭!

See the fingering summary below for these fingerings, for two octave arpeggios.

ROOT POSITION ARPEGGIO FINGERING SUMMARY
(Ascending fingering only)

MAJORS:				D	A	E	B	F♯	R.H. 1231235 L.H. 5321321
	F	C	G						R.H. 1231235 L.H. 5421421
MINORS:	E♭	F	C	G	D	A	E	B	R.H. 1231235 L.H. 5421421
MAJORS:		D♭	A♭	E♭					R.H. 2124124 L.H. 2142142
MINORS:	F♯	D♭	A♭						R.H. 2124124 L.H. 2142142
MAJOR:	B♭								R.H. 2124124 L.H. 3213213
MINOR:	B♭								R.H. 2312312 L.H. 3213213

For Example.
D♭ Major
Arpeggio

THE HARMONIC SERIES

When we hear a single note on a Clarinet or on the Piano, we are instantly able to tell which instrument is playing the note. The reason for this is that, apart from the fundamental note that is being played, we also hear a series of Harmonics or upper Partials (parts of the note) and each instrument favours some of these more than others. This alters the tone colour of the instrument so that a Trumpet sounds different to a Violin and so on.

It is through the knowledge and use of these Upper Partials that our whole system (the Western System) of tuning is evolved.

The system is based upon the interval of an Octave. Experiments were made on the sound of a bowed string (such as that on a violin). The fundamental note produced by the full length of the string was found to move up by an octave if the string was stopped at the mid-point. In other words only half of the string length was vibrating, the way it would if the violinist held the string down with his left hand while bowing with the right hand. When the string was stopped at the 2/3rds point, it sounded an Octave and a Fifth higher (a twelfth). As the string is stopped at various points, therefore, the string lengths form, what algebra books call a 'Harmonical Progression', or 'Harmonic Series'.

The same phenomenon occurs when playing a Brass Instrument such as a trumpet. As the player exerts more wind and lip pressure the notes move up the Harmonic Series of the Fundamental note that is being fingered.

The series always follow the same intervallic sequence:

HARMONIC SERIES (Fundamental C)

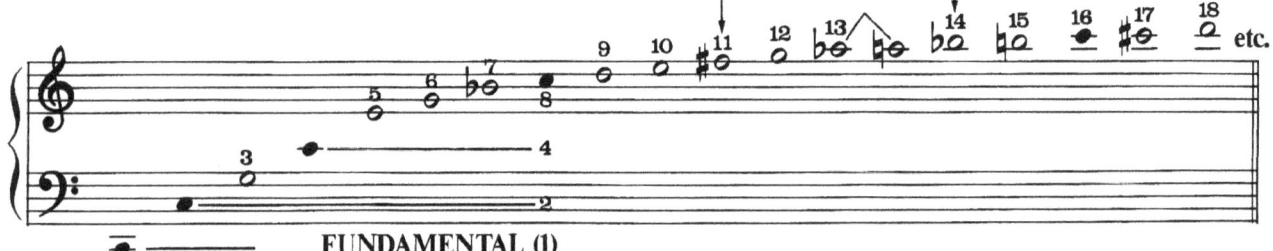

N.B. Harmonics 1, 2, 4, 8, 16, 32 etc. = same name as fundamental.

This explains why the Bugle call always uses the notes of the Major Triad. The bugle has no valves, so that it can only play the Harmonic Series of one note, its Fundamental. The Fundamental note is dependent on the length and width of the tubing. A Trombone sounds lower than a Trumpet because it is a larger instrument and has more tubing.

The tone colour of the various instruments as mentioned previously, is affected by which Harmonics an instrument favours. Some favour the even Harmonics (2, 4, 6, 8 etc and some favour the odd Harmonics 3, 5, 7 etc.)

For instance the Saxophone favours the even Harmonics while the Clarinet filters out the even Harmonics leaving only the Odd Harmonics to sound.

The Harmonic Series plays a very important part in the way the Indian instrument the Sitar (played by Ravi Shankar) operates. The instrument has 7 played strings and numerous (13) sympathetic strings run under the frets. As each string is played, any of those sympathetic strings tuned to the Harmonic Series of the played note, are also set in motion. This gives the Sitar its special 'buzzing' sound.

On a Piano we can usually only hear the lower Harmonics of the series. To do this, play two 'Cs' one octave apart in the lower register of the keyboard with the sustain pedal depressed prior to playing. Then listen carefully as the notes die away. You should be able to hear the 5th and 6th Harmonics (E & G) as well as the C's. You will probably not be able to distinguish the 4th harmonic (C) as a separate note. If the piano is particularly good or the acoustics of the room are favourable you may be able to hear a few of the higher Harmonics as well.

THE PENTATONIC SCALE

As seen on page 10 the first two harmonics in the series, the ones that most people can hear without too much trouble, are at intervals of an octave an an octave and a fifth. As a result the music of many regions of the world uses scales made up of these intervals. When a progression of 5 intervals of a fifth is put together as a scale, the resulting scale is known as a Pentatonic Scale. (From Penta meaning five and ton meaning note or sound). For example these notes which are a fifth apart. C, G, D, A, E can be arranged to form a scale C, D, E, G, A. The Pentatonic scale can be heard in the music of such countries as Scotland, England, Ireland, Japan, China, Indonesia, the folk music of America particularly the Negro spirituals and so on.

Here is a Pentatonic song for you to play. Add your own Left Hand accompaniment, using the chords as a guide. Add 6ths and 7ths to the basic chord according to your own taste. Style the accompaniment on one of the suggestions in Book 2 of this series.

2. SWING LOW SWEET CHARIOT

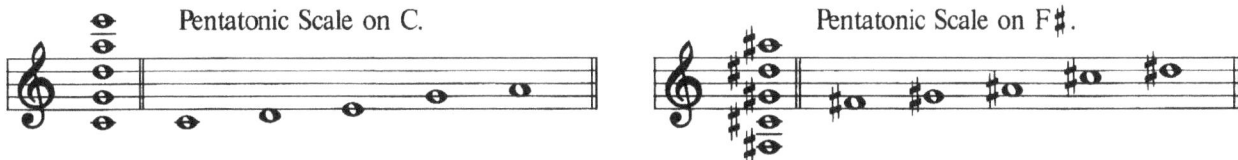

Other well-known pentatonic tunes to listen for are: Git along, little dogies and The Lone Star trail (both Traditional cow-boy songs); Deep River and Little David (Negro Spirituals); Liza Jane and the Mocking Bird song (Southern Folksongs); Auld Lang Syne and Ye Banks and Ye Braes (Scottish) and My Bonnie Couckoo. (Irish).

3. BELLS OF BUDDHA

TECHNIQUE TIP: To play the left-hand figure (bars 1–10, 18–20) keep the left-hand outstretched and, using the third finger as a fixed pivot-point, angle the wrist to the left for the low note, and to the right for the higher notes.

Moderato

Margaret S. Brandman

IMPROVISATION

Using the Pentatonic scale, improvise a short piece, listening to the effects created by the use of the sustain pedal.

HARMONY

The Harmonic Series provides us with the aural reason for not doubling the third degree of the Major Triad. Most traditional Harmony books advise that the Root and Fifth of a chord may be doubled but not the third. Most books neglect to mention the reason. The reason is that the 5th harmonic is quite a strong harmonic. When playing the Root and 5th notes only, the Major third is also faintly audible. If the third were to be doubled it would in effect sound as if it were being 'tripled' and would therefore tend to take on the acoustical sound as the Fundamental Note of the triad. This would set up a clash of tonalities between the played Root Note and the acoustical Root Note. That is, in a C major triad, the E would take on the sound as the Root Note of the triad. You would then have the Harmonic series on E (which includes a G♯) clashing with the Harmonic series of C.

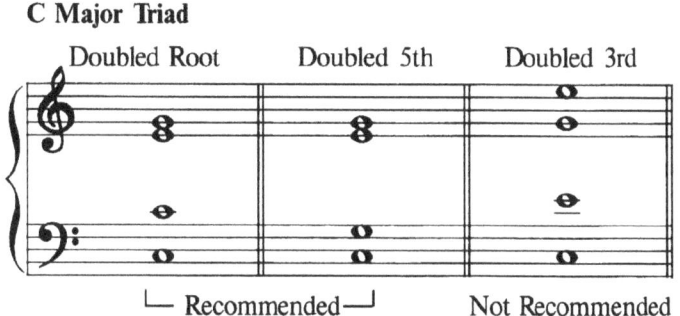

The Eleventh Harmonic

One other important harmonic to keep in mind, is the Eleventh Harmonic. This note is closer in sound to F♯ than to F Natural (in the C series). Owing to this fact, the F♯ creates a better blend of sound in some of the extended chords, for instance the Major 13th chord, than the Natural version of the note would. There will be more discussion on this aspect of extended chords in Book Four.

The Harmonic Series Scale. There is also a scale, used by many Jazz musicians and serious Contemporary composers, which is formed from the notes of the Harmonic series. The scale is known to Jazz players as either the Lydian Scale with a Flattened 7th, or a Mixolydian scale with a Sharpened 4th. The scale suits the Dominant 9♯11 Chord or the Dominant 13♯11 chord. c.f. Jazz Scales in Book Four.

The so-called 'mystic' chord of the composer Alexander Scriabin (1872-1915) is built of superimposed 4ths using notes taken from the scale, or viewing them another way, taken directly from the upper partials of the harmonic series.

PLAY AND LISTEN TO THE FOLLOWING EXAMPLES.

REALIZATION OF A FIGURED BASS

If you refer to page 62 in Book 2 of this series, you will recall that realization of a Figured Bass was discussed as part of the section on Chord Naming systems. Several pages in Book 3 will be devoted to developing your ability to play a Figured Bass line, supplying (realizing) the remaining notes in the right hand part.

The figuring for the triads is as follows: (a) the full figuring with the numbers that are understood in brackets and (b) the standard figuring used, with the numbers that are understood being omitted.

(a)	Root Position Triad	First Inversion	Second Inversion
	(5)	6	6
	(3)	(3)	4

(b)	—	6	6
			4

FIGURED BASS EXERCISES SECTION ONE
ROOT POSITION

As you can see from the above chart, if a Root Position chord is required, no figuring will appear under the bass note. A Bass progression such as this —

would be realized by supplying the correct chord from the table in three-note form in the Right hand. The note that is usually doubled is the Root note. Unless the top note of the chord is given, there could be several arrangements of the Right Hand part, depending upon which inversion is used to commence the phrase.

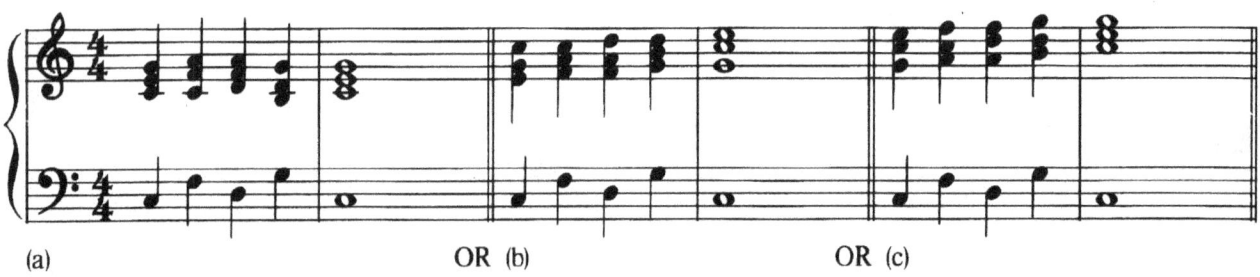

(a)　　　　　　　　OR (b)　　　　　　　OR (c)

In the following exercises, supply the missing 2 notes to each chord, placing them under the given melody notes. Before playing each exercise, complete the chord table for the key so that you will know which type (Major or Minor etc) of chord to use. Double the Root note in each chord, except in the chord movement from V to vi or vi to V in which case the **third** must be **doubled in chord vi** to avoid *consecutive octaves or fifths with chord V. If it is not possible or practical to play the doubled third it can be implied. To imply the doubled third in piano style, play only the third and the fifth of the chord in the right hand.

*Refer to *Harmony Comes Together* by Margaret Brandman.

CHORD TABLE

Exercise 1

CHORD TABLE

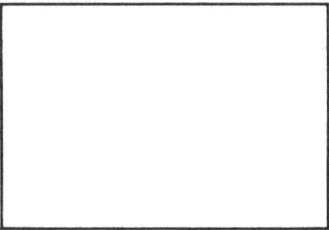

Do not forget to raise the seventh degree in a minor key, so that the dominant chord will be a major triad.

*Accidentals: Refer to page 40 — Altered Chords.

Exercise 2

CHROMATIC CHORDS

A Chromatic Chord is one that contains notes foreign to the Key Signature in which the piece is written. It can be built on a note foreign to the scale or it can have altered notes within the structure of the chord. For instance, any chord built on the note E♭, when the piece is in C Major, would be a Chromatic chord in that key. Likewise, a D7th chord (D, F♯, A, C) is a Chromatic chord in key of C Major, because of the F sharp.

There are Two Chromatic chords which are historically very important to our study of Jazz Progressions. These chords are built on the Flattened 6th and Flattened 2nd notes of the major scale. They have been used in many classical pieces from the time of J.S. Bach (1700's) onwards. They are also the most likely chords, other than those in the table, to pop up in a piece of music that has not actually changed key.

(1) The Chromatic Chord built on the Flattened 6th degree of the scale, is likely to occur in three forms. To distinguish them from one another, Classical theorists have given them the names: 'Italian' 6th, 'German' 6th, and 'French' 6th respectively. The basic construction of all three forms is a Major 3rd interval from the Root note and a 'Sharpened 6th', (or Augmented 6th) interval from the Root note. Hence the name '6th Chords'.

The Italian 6th chord consists of only these intervals, (a three-note chord); the German 6th has a Perfect 5th interval from the root note, in addition to the other intervals (a four-note chord); and the French 6th has a Flattened 5th (Diminished 5th) interval from the root note in addition to the basic structure. (Also a four-note chord.) See Example 1.

Example 1   **CHROMATIC CHORDS**

Listen to the sound of all three chords. The German 6th sounds just like a Dominant 7th chord and the Italian 6th sounds almost the same — minus one note. The French 6th sounds a little more exotic because of the Flattened 5th interval.

Remember, however, that none of these chords functions as a Dominant seventh. All are written as 6th chords, and it is this 'spelling' of the chord that is your clue to understanding its function in the piece. In most cases the chord will resolve onto the chord on the Fifth Degree of the Major Scale and from there the progression will move on to the Tonic Chord. (See Example 2 for the usual movement of these chords.) At no time will the chord function as a Dominant 7th, when it is written as a German 6th.

Example 2

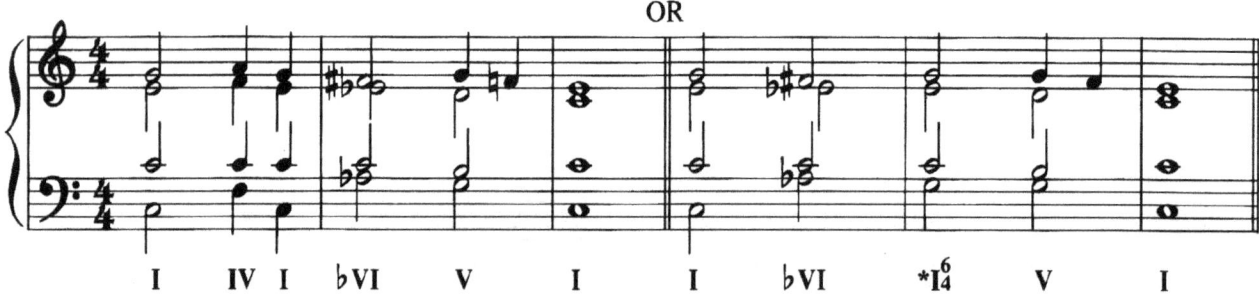

*Second Inversion — Bass Note is still V.

(2) The Chromatic Chord built on the flattened 2nd degree of the scale, has one form only and is known as the Neapolitan 6th chord. It is usually found in the First Inversion and is in fact a plain Major Chord. The intervals from the Bass note are a Minor 3rd and a Minor 6th. Often the Bass note is repeated in the voicing of the chord to produce a four-note chord. The basic structure however remains a three-note chord.

The resolution of this chord will come about in the same way as the resolutions for the German 6th, moving to the chord built on the fifth degree of the scale and from there to the Tonic chord of the key. (See Example 3).

Example 3

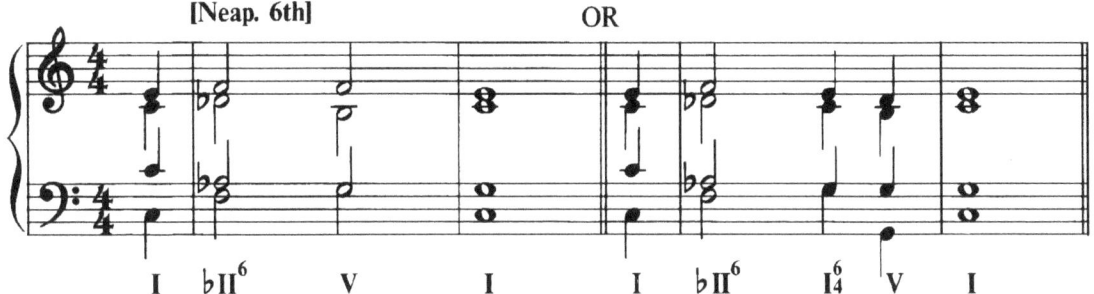

I   ♭II⁶   V   I   I   ♭II⁶   I⁶₄   V   I

The use of any of these chords can lend an element of pleasant surprise to much of the music written before 1900. If you hear something a little unusual, chances are that it is a French 6th or the like. Be on the lookout (and listen-out) for these chords in every piece you play. Add these chords to the table of chords that you write for each piece you play. (See Example 4.) Also note that because these chords are 'artificial' chords to the key in which they occur, they are exactly the same in both **major** and **minor** keys. In the Minor Key both the Major triad on the sixth degree (in C Minor it would be A♭ Major chord) and the Italian, German, or French 6ths are built on the same note. (No need to Flatten the sixth degree any further, as it is already Flattened for the Minor Scale.)

Example 4

EXTENDED TABLES

MAJOR			MINOR		
IV	I	V	iv	i	V
ii	vi	iii	VI	III	ii⁰
		vii⁰			vii⁰
♭II - Neapolitan 6th			♭II - Neapolitan 6th		
♭VI - It. Germ. & Fr. 6th			♭VI - It. Germ. & Fr. 6ths		
EXAMPLE IN C MAJOR			**EXAMPLE IN C MINOR**		
F	C	G	Fm	Cm	G
Dm	Am	Em	A♭	E♭	D⁰
		B⁰			B⁰
♭II - D♭ Neapolitan 6th			♭II - D♭ Neapolitan 6th		
♭VI - A♭ It. Germ. & Fr. 6ths			♭VI - A♭ It. Germ. & Fr. 6ths		

Refer to the Advanced Modulation Spider Chart on page 20 which includes extended tables.
Spider Chart templates for both Major and Minor keys can be found in
Contemporary Piano Method Book 2B.

HANDY MANUSCRIPT

CHORD ANALYSIS BY DEGREE NUMBERS

During the course of the three books in this method, chords have been treated from several points of view. Most often, the chord has been named according to its Modern Chord name and has then been correlated with its numerical position in the chord table. If you have been writing in the chord names for each piece played you should by now be quite familiar with both the chord name and the position it occupies in the scale and the progression.

To take the analysis a stage further, simply write the degree numbers under each bar, to match the chord symbol you have already written above.

This style of analysis is very useful for viewing chord progressions in general rather than viewing specific chords tied to specific keys or pieces. The style is used both by students of classical music and by students of Jazz. Jazz students in particular use the system to compare similar types of progression in varying standard tunes, and to learn structures of songs so that they can be easily transposed from key to key. (cf The John Mehegan books on Jazz Piano).

The chord progression below is the first eight bars of 'You are the Sunshine of My Life' by Stevie Wonder. The Modern Chord names are written above the staff, while the degree numbers are placed below the staff.

YOU ARE THE SUNSHINE OF MY LIFE

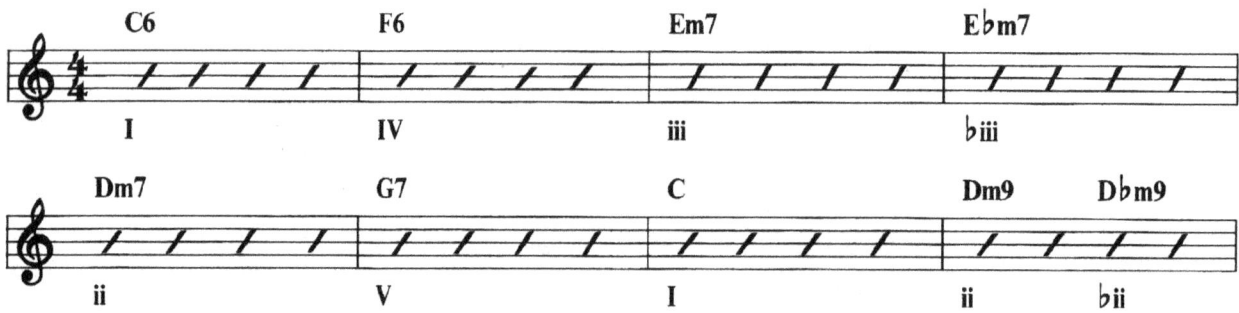

This popular Prelude by Chopin is the basis for the song 'Could this be the Magic' by Barry Manilow. Even after 150 years, the beautiful chord sequence still fascinates the listener.

The Left-Hand octaves have been fingered with finger-swaps so that you can feel your way from octave to octave without having to look down at your hands. Keep this technique in mind when similar octave passages occur in other pieces you wish to play.

Before playing the piece, work out the full Chord Table, including the Chromatic Sixth chords, and write it out in the space provided. Next, write the chord names above each bar and indicate the degree numbers below each bar as shown in Bar 1. Place an asterisk beside the degree number of any Chromatic Sixth chords you find, and mark them as either Italian (It) German (Gmn), French (F), or Neopolitan (Neap) sixths. Remember that these chords are only found on the Flattened 6th and Flattened 2nd degrees of the scale.

You will no doubt notice some interesting extension notes added to a few of the chords. Refer to the sections on extended chords in the latter section of this book and in Book Four, or to Book Two of the Contemporary Chord Workbook series by Margaret S. Brandman.

4. PRELUDE
CHORD TABLE

ADVANCED MODULATION SPIDER FOR A PIECE IN A MAJOR KEY

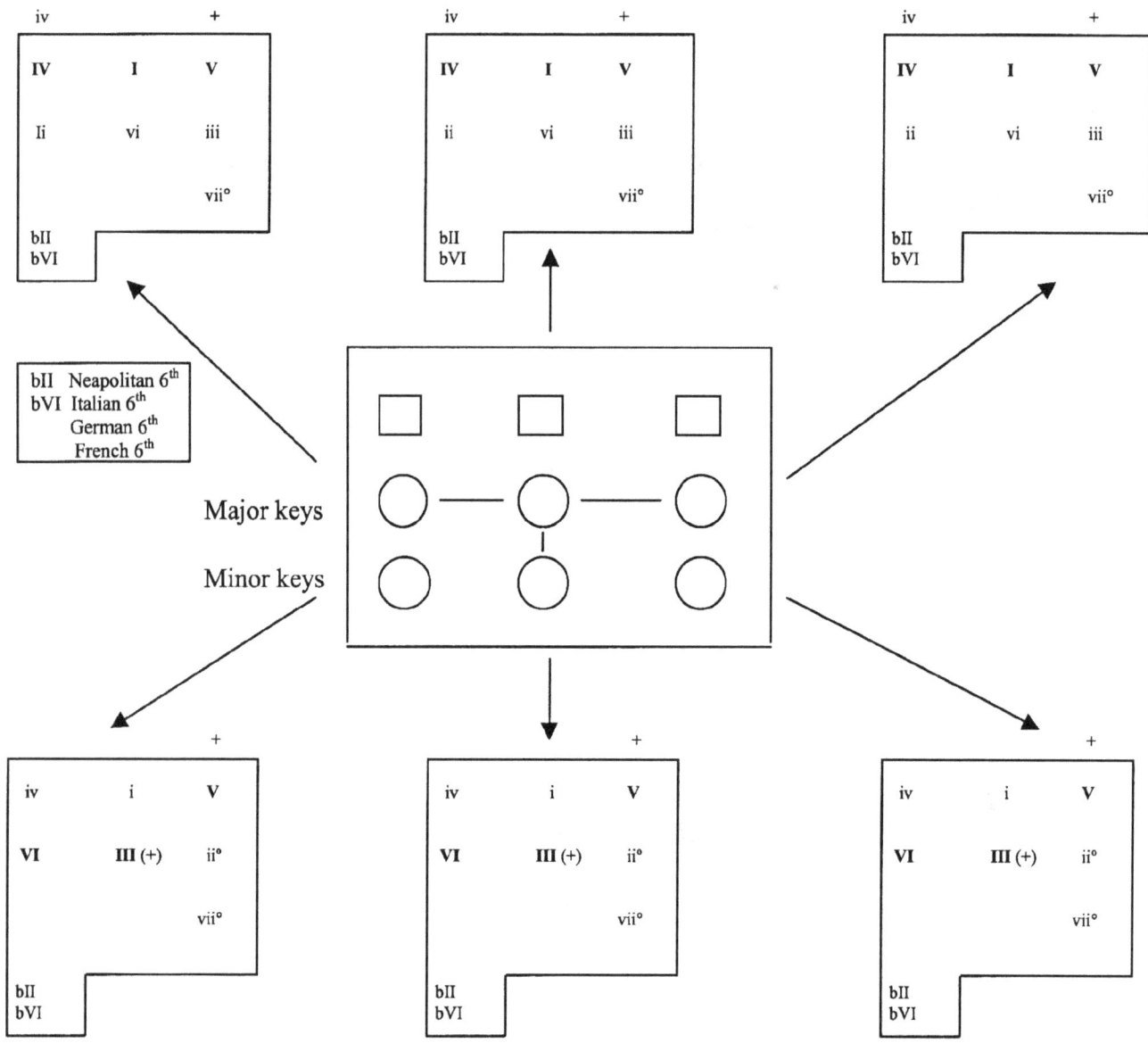

Colour Coding

When analysing any piece, you can colour code the keys by choosing one colour for each of the six keys. Add colour to each of the key centre circles.

Remember to place the *number* of sharps or flats for each key signature in the boxes.

Use this Modulation Spider Chart as a template. Owners of this book are permitted to photocopy this page for use with pieces in different keys. Refer to Contemporary Piano Method Book 2B for the Advanced Modulation Spider Chart for minor keys.

© Copyright Dr. Margaret Brandman 2002

CANON

The word Canon is derived from the Greek word *κανών* meaning 'rule' or 'standard'. Therefore a Canon is a piece of music written strictly according to rule.

The basic idea of a Canon is that of imitation. A melody begun in one voice or part, is imitated note-for-note at a few beats distance, either at the same or at a different pitch, in a similar manner to a 'round', (remember 'Frere Jacques').

There are many types of canons including retrograde (going backwards) and inverse (inverted). An interesting type of canon is the Crab Canon also known as canon 'Cancrizans' (from the latin word *Cancer* meaning crab).

In a Crab Canon the notes are the same whether they are written forwards or backwards. An example of a Crab Canon can be found in the book titled Baroque Piano Styles, edited by Joseph Castle (Mel Bay pub).

5. AROUND SEVEN
(Canon)

Margaret S. Brandman

INVERSION FINGERINGS FOR MAJOR AND MINOR TRIAD ARPEGGIOS

If you refer back to page 9 you will recall that the fingering for all Root Position arpeggios, major and minor was discussed. To compete the section on arpeggios, presented below are the remaining fingerings for the inversions of these arpeggios.

For F, C, G & F♯ Major arpeggios and for D, A, E & E♭ minor arpeggios use the following fingerings:

	ROOT	First Inversion	Second Inversion
Right Hand	1 2 3 5	1 2 4 5	1 2 4 5
Left Hand	*5 4 2 1	5 4 2 1	5 3 2 1

As you can see, the fingering for two of the positions in either hand, is the same.
*For this position in F♯ Major arpeggio, use the 3rd finger instead of the 4th.

For D, A and E Major arpeggios use:

	ROOT	First Inversion	Second Inversion
Right Hand	1 2 3 5	2 *1 2 4	*1 2 4 5
Left Hand	5 3 2 *1	3 2 *1 3	5 3 2 1

N.B. The thumbs are on the same note in those inversions marked with an asterisk (*).

For F, C and G. Minor arpeggios use:

	ROOT	First Inversion	Second Inversion
Right Hand	1 2 3 5	3 *1 2 3	*1 2 3 5
Left Hand	5 4 2 *1	4 2 *1 4	5 3 2 1

For B♭ Major arpeggio use.

	ROOT	First Inversion	Second Inversion
Right Hand	2 *1 2 4	*1 2 4 5	1 2 4 5
Left Hand	3 2 *1 3	5 4 2 1	5 3 2 *1

For B Minor arpeggio use:

	ROOT	First Inversion	Second Inversion
Right Hand	*1 2 3 5	1 2 4 5	3 *1 2 3
Left Hand	5 4 2 1	5 4 2 *1	4 2 *1 4

In order to travel more than one octave, repeat the fingering given remembering to replace the fifth finger with the Thumb where applicable, as was done for Arpeggios in Root Position.

For all those arpeggios with only **one white note**, the basic Root Position fingering is retained, while the arpeggio is begun on either the 2nd or 3rd note depending on the inversion required. This is done so that the thumb always lands on the white note. This applies to the following arpeggios:

Majors — B, D♭, A♭, E♭.
Minors — F♯, C♯, (D♭), A♭, B♭.
See Example 3.

Example 3

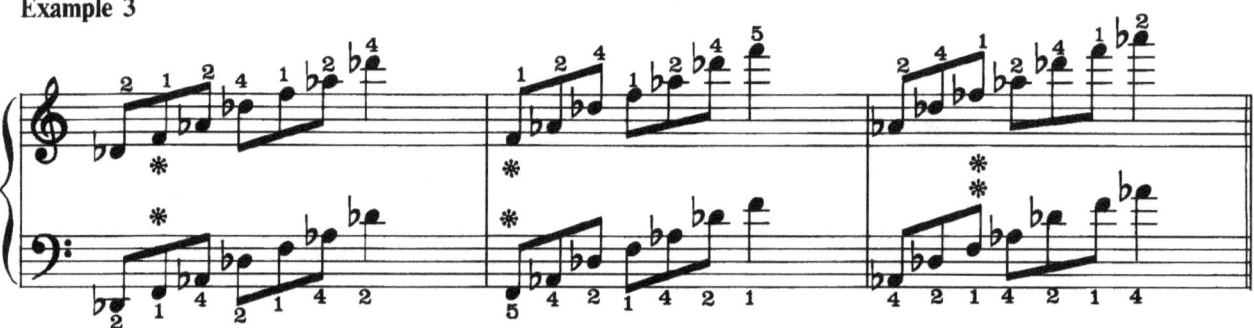

TECHNIQUE TIPS

Remember the following technique tips for playing arpeggios.

(1) Angle the arms with elbows away from the body so that the thumbs are more easily able to pass under the other fingers and conversely, so that the fingers can cross over more easily when moving in the other direction.

Example 4

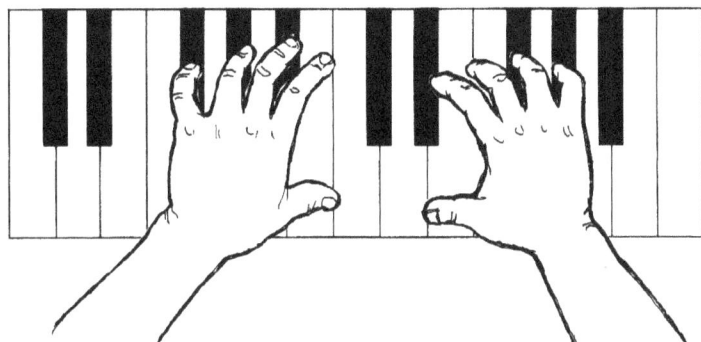

(2) Play the arpeggios at first over two octaves then extend the range to three and later four octaves. Each of these arpeggios may be accented in threes, so that the notes with the same name as the starting note are accented each time. However, when playing the arpeggio over four octaves, it is wiser to accent in groups of four. By doing this you will be accenting a different note name each time so that all the fingers are used equally. This also prevents a tendency to drop the wrists each time the thumb is played and adds to the smoothness of the sound of the arpeggio. See Example 5.

Example 5

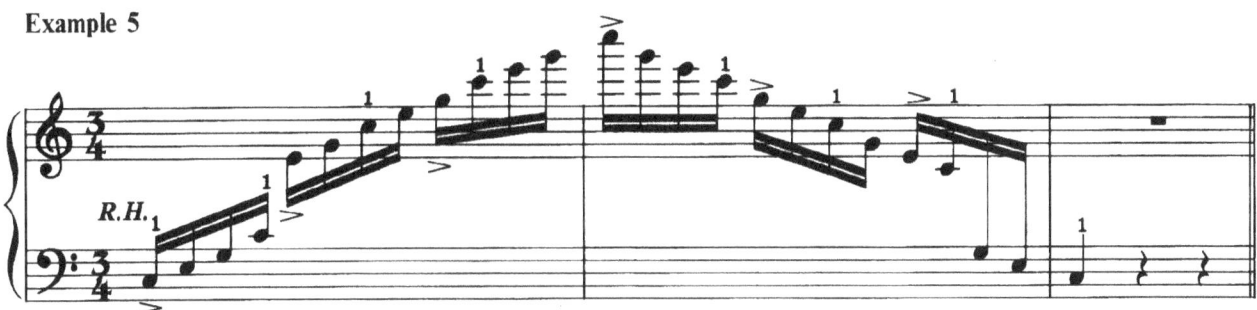

(3) Keep the hands at a slightly higher position than when playing scales to facilitate the movement of the thumb under the other fingers and allow the other fingers to be placed correctly on the black notes.

6. FLYING HIGH (Arpeggio Study)

This study uses all 24 Major and Minor triad arpeggios.

Before playing the piece, be sure to write in the chord names above the bars, so that you will have had a close look at the structure of the music, and will therefore be mentally prepared for each change of chord and hand-position.

Use the sustain pedal sparingly throughout, making sure to clear the pedal at each chord change.

For further technique studies, refer to the works of the three 'C's: Muzio Clementi (Gradus ad Parnassum), John Cramer (84 Studies) and Carl Czerny (The School of Velocity, Op. 299 and The Art of Finger Dexterity, Op 740.)

6. FLYING HIGH

Margaret S. Brandman

Vivace

ALTERED CHORDS

If you have studied the material in Book 2 of this series by now you should know all the basic four-note chords used in Pop and Jazz tunes. They are the Major and Minor 6th chords and Major, Minor, Dominant, Diminished and Minor 7♭5 (Half-Diminished) Seventh chords and the Dominant 7 suspended 4th chord usually written Dominant 7 sus.

The reason I call these the basic chords is that you are required to know the construction of these chords as the chord name itself has no real clues as to how the chord is built. (For instance, you won't find a Minor 6th chord by taking the 1st, 3rd, 5th and 6th note from the ordinary Harmonic Minor scale).

However once you understand the construction of these chords it is easy enough to follow a direction such as 'sharpen the 7th' or 'flatten the 5th'.

The two most frequently used altered 7th chords are the Dominant 7♯5 and the Dominant 7♭5 chords.

THE DOMINANT SEVENTH ♯5 CHORD incorporates the Augmented Triad and is frequently used because of this sound, as a replacement for the straight Dominant seventh chord. (see Example 1).

Example 1

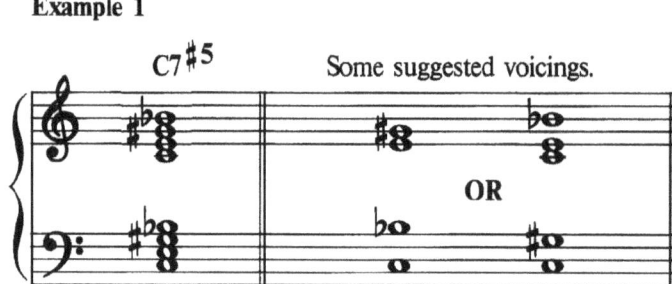

THE DOMINANT SEVENTH ♭5 CHORD is in fact the French 6th chord sound mentioned on page 16. This is another example of a 'two-in-one' chord. When you reach the second inversion of the chord it can be seen as a Dominant 7♭5th chord on the new Root Note. (see Example 2).

C7♭5 = G♭7♭5 and vice versa. As a result there are only six of these chord shapes.

Example 2a

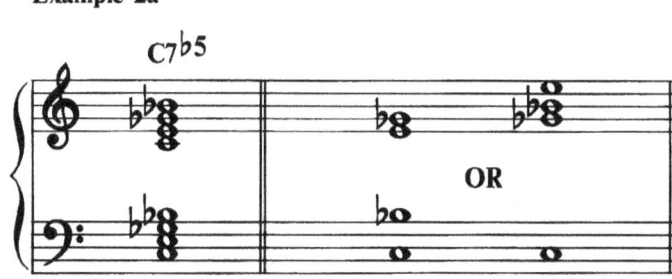

Example 2b

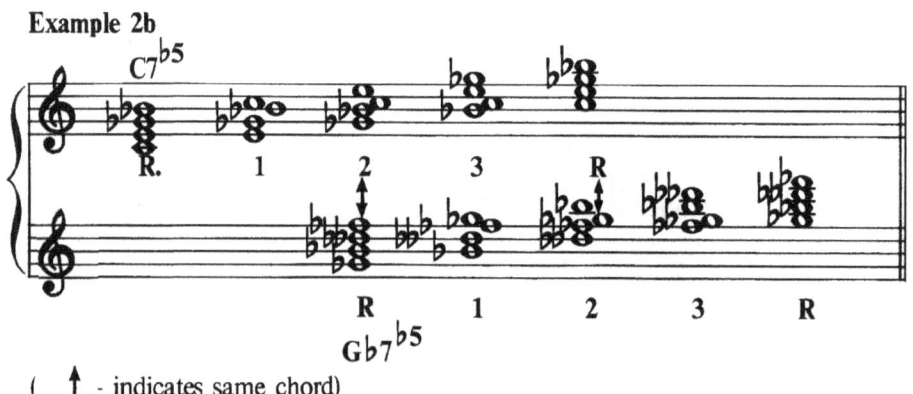

(↕ - indicates same chord)

Example 3a

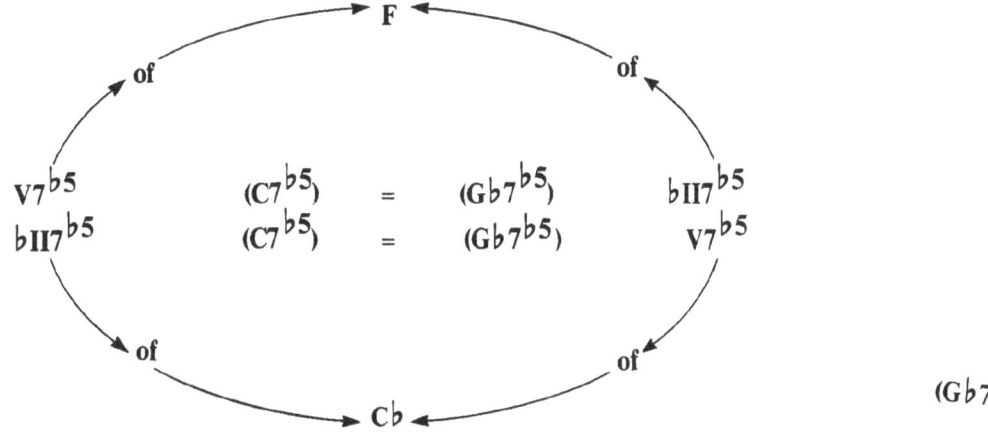

If you refer to page 44 you will see that both these chords can lead back to the same key. $C7\flat5$ would lead back to F as its Dominant 7th and $G\flat7\flat5$ would lead back to F from its position as the Flattened 2nd degree of the scale. (Step 11 Root Progressions, substituting the Flattened 2nd for the Dominant 7th.)

Likewise $G\flat7\flat5$ would lead back to $C\flat$ Major (or Minor) as its Dominant Chord and $C\flat7\flat5$ would lead back to $C\flat$ Major from its position as the Flattened 2nd degree of the scale. (See Example 3).

This type of chord therefore, makes an excellent pivot chord, facilitating modulation to distant keys.

Example 3b

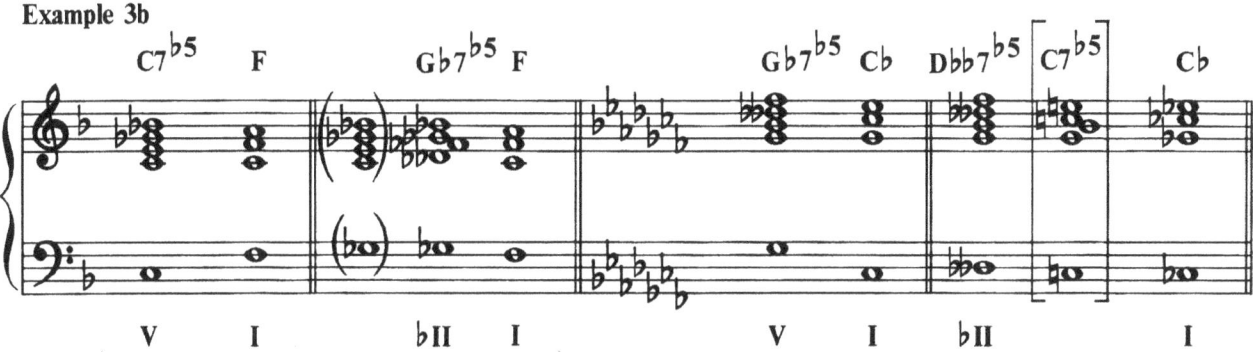

Practise these chords in all twelve keys (remember they can apply to both Major and Minor Keys). Once you are familiar with them use the Altered chords to provide colour to your playing. Use them in the Blues progressions given on the following pages as replacement chords for the Dominant 7ths.

WRITE CHORD TABLES FOR No. 7 TRAVELLIN' SONG IN THE SPACE BELOW.

7. TRAVELLIN' SONG

Before playing this piece write the chord names above the bars, so that you can analyse the chord movements.

To count $\frac{11}{16}$ time divide the bars into sub-groups of two's and three's. Use the space on the previous page to draw up Chord Tables for each key.

Margaret S. Brandman

MORE ALTERED CHORDS

Three other altered chords occasionally used to add aural colour and interest to a chord progression are the altered Major 7th chords; Major 7♯5 (sharpened 5th), Major 7♭5 (flattened 5th), and the altered Minor chord; Minor ♯7 (Minor triad with a sharpened 7th).

(1) a and b. The MAJOR 7th chord can use the altered notes of a sharpened or flattened 5th. The Major 7 ♯5 has the sound of an Augmented chord and is a very bright colour. It can be built up on the 3rd degree of the Harmonic Minor scale.

The MAJOR 7♭5 is a little more unusual again. The chord shape is more often found as the top end of a Dominant 9 (13) chord. (see Book Four.)

Both chords are used in many contemporary jazz and jazz-rock pieces, for instance the music of Steely Dan, and can be found in the music of Bartok and Kabalevsky to mention a few of the serious composers of the Twentieth Century.

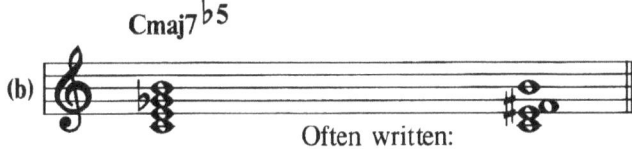

(2) The Minor Triad can be used with a Major 7th interval added to it, rather than the more usual minor 7th interval. The symbol used is 'm♯7'. This chord can be found as the Tonic 7th chord in the Harmonic Minor scale.

As such, this chord can be used as a final chord in a minor piece of music. It is also often used in a progression in which a melodic line moves in falling semitones over a constant triad. For instance, Dm (D top note), Dm♯7, Dm7, Dm6. The chords can be used also to set up a counter line to the original melody. A good example of the use of this progression is the tune 'Gentle On My Mind'. Another example is the tune 'Music To Watch Girls Go By'.

Play all of these chords on all twelve notes in the octave. Practice them in inversions in both Block and Broken forms.

FIGURED BASS EXERCISES — SECTION 2

FIRST INVERSION CHORDS

When arranging a First Inversion chord for piano style continue to double the Root note. As the 3rd degree is taken by the bass, the notes remaining for the Right Hand part are two Root notes and one 5th. Thus:

Alternatively, the Right Hand can play 2 fifths and only one Root note, or even only one each of the 3rd and 5th degrees, the extra note being implied. Thus:

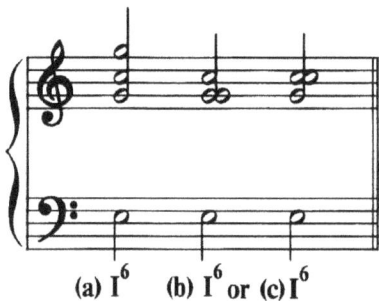

If two First Inversion chords are played a second apart, consecutive octaves and fifths can be avoided by omitting one of the Root notes or one of the fifths in each alternate chord. Thus:

DIMINISHED TRIADS

Diminished triads in Root position are avoided owing to the harsh sound of the chord. Therefore, the triad is usually played in the First Inversion and sometimes in the Second Inversion, unless it is part of a sequence.

When playing a Diminished triad, any note OTHER THAN the ROOT can be doubled. An easy rule of thumb, therefore is to play one of each (1st, 3rd and 5th) in the Right Hand if the chord is in either First or Second Inversion.

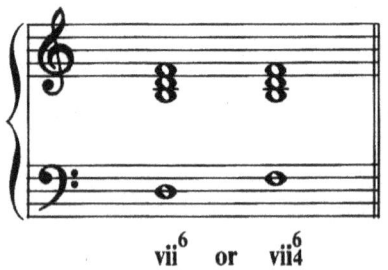

EXERCISES

After completing the chord tables, play the following exercises. If you wish, write the chord names above the bar and the chord degree numbers below the bass notes.

CHORD TABLE

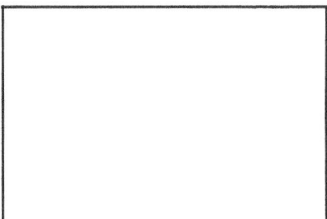

Exercise 1

CHORD TABLE

Exercise 2

ROOT PROGRESSIONS
STEP ONE

One of the themes of Books Three and Four will be the study of Root Progressions and the application of substitute chords, through a knowledge of Root Progressions.

After each progression has been discussed it will be applied in a 12-bar blues format. This provides a framework for the progression and gives the chord movement a definite direction.

The principles inherent in the progressions, nevertheless can be applied not only to a blues progression but also to many varied musical styles and compositions.

The first Step in this process is to substitute a series of chords, on Roots taken from the 'Cycle of Fifths', for the existing simple Blues changes, (chords). In such a pattern, the first four bars would be the Tonic (I) chord of the key, followed by two bars of the Subdominant (IV) chord. It is this Subdominant chord which becomes the first Goal chord. All the Substituted chords must lead logically to this Subdominant chord.

BASIC TWELVE-BAR BLUES PATTERN

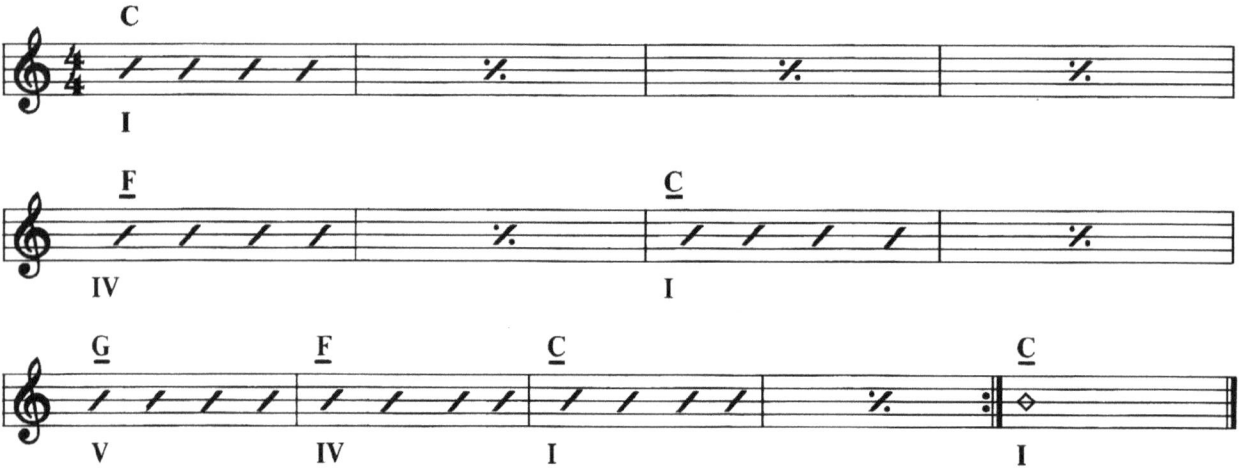

Let us, for this reason, work backwards from our Goal chord. The chord that leads best into this goal chord is its Dominant Seventh chord. The Root note of this Dominant Seventh chord is a fifth higher than the goal chord. If we play the Dominant Seventh for the last two beats of bar four, we can then substitute another chord for the first two beats of this bar. Once again we can use its Dominant Seventh as the best leading chord. The Root note will again be a Fifth higher than the chord it leads into. Thus we could work our way backwards, with each chord being the Dominant Seventh of the next and occupying two beats in each bar. If we leave our original Tonic chord on the first two beats of Bar 1, we find that the next chord seems to 'jump' up the cycle of fifths to the sharpened fourth degree of the scale. This is because we have cut the cycle short as we only had four bars to travel. If you know your cycle you will have already realised that you would need to travel right around the twelve chords of the cycle to end up exactly where you started from.

Thus the progression ends up looking like this:— I, ♯IV, VII, III, VI, II, V, I with the last 'I' being the Dominant Seventh of the Subdominant chord needed in Bar 5. See Example 1. Notice how the Left Hand Root progression moves in falling fifth intervals. (When inverted they become rising 4ths). The starting place in each case has a box around the chord and the 'Goal' chords have been underlined. Remember it is always recommended to work backwards from the 'goal' chord. Later on you will know just how much time you have, (two bars or four bars etc.), and how much of the cycle progression to use. However for the moment work these progressions out on paper and at the keyboard. (See Examples 1 and 2).

Extended Stem: Supply remainder of chord under the given note.

Example 2

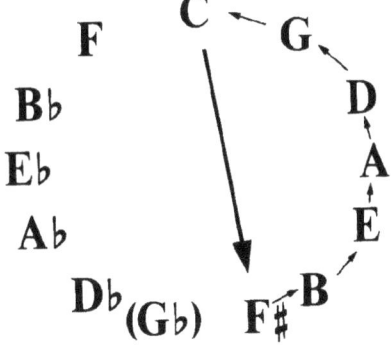

Once you understand the principle involved, (each Dominant Seventh leading on to the next), you can then take each Root Note and vary the quality of the Seventh built on it. When the progression is played using all Dominant Seventh Chords it sounds quite 'square' even quite Classical; to jazz it up a bit, try placing Minor 7th, Major 7th, Minor 7♭5th, Major 6th and Minor 6th chords above the root notes as well as the Dominant 7ths. Mix and match them, experiment, and above all play the sounds and listen to the various effects that the different chord qualities lend to the progression. **N.B.** Make sure that the chord in the 'boxed' position remains a Dominant 7th for the moment. Also do not use Diminished seventh chords at this stage as they require special resolutions.

A good chord to use straight after the Tonic chord at the beginning of the progression, is the Minor 7♭5 chord, as it has only one note altered from the Tonic chord. (See Example 3). If you work your progression out using mainly Minor 7th chords in the first half of the bar followed by Dominant 7th chords in the second half of the bar, you will have what is seen in many jazz books as II-V progressions. See bars 3 and 4 of Example 3.

Example 4. I have suggested three different pianistic styles in which to practise the progressions. The first has the left hand playing the Root note and the right hand providing the chord. The second has both hands playing the chord and the third has the left hand playing the chord and the right hand picking a melody note from each chord to provide a singing line over the progression. It is this third style which can later be added to, as an improvised right hand melody.

Do not forget to work out the progressions in other keys. Write one in each of the twelve keys if you have time.

Example 4

Style 1 — Use when accompanying a soloist or singer without a bass player. The left hand is often played an octave lower than it is written.

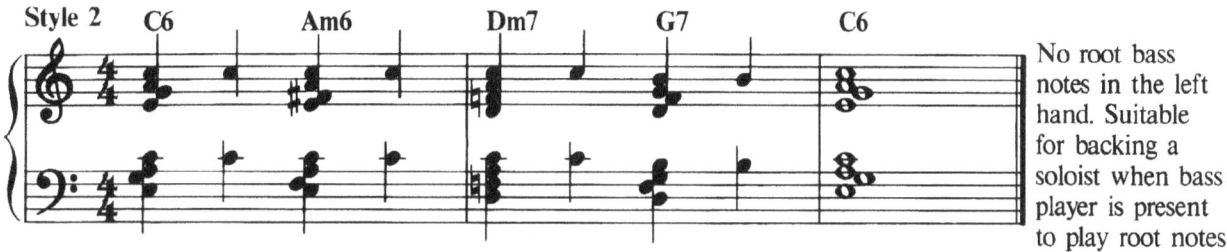

Style 2 — No root bass notes in the left hand. Suitable for backing a soloist when bass player is present to play root notes.

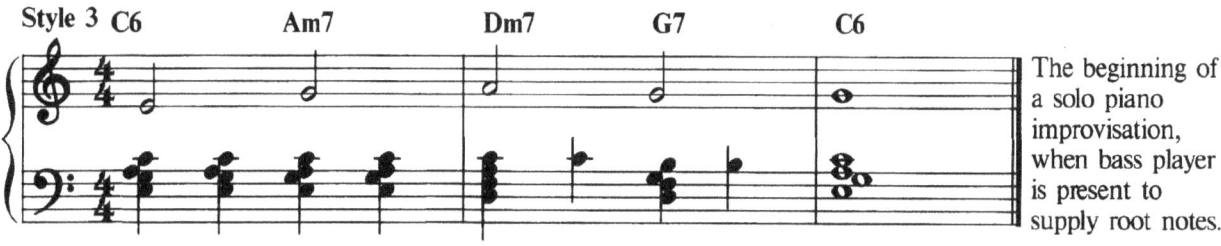

Style 3 — The beginning of a solo piano improvisation, when bass player is present to supply root notes.

A suggested supplementary piece for performance which demonstrates a Cycle of Fifths progression is the piece 'Weaving' from the book DREAMWEAVING (Five Chord Studies for Contemporary Pianists) by Margaret Brandman

8. ALLEGRO FROM EASY DIVERTIMENTO

Joseph Haydn
Arr. for C Clef by M.S. Brandman

INVENTION

The term 'Invention' was a special term coined by J.S. Bach to name his works for 2 voices (parts) in Binary Form.

In the writing of these pieces Bach was indeed being 'inventive' using basic canonic and imitative ideas and using as little material as possible, Bach plays with the material in many different ways to create an interesting yet cohesive piece of music.

He makes use of Sequence (repetition of the same melodic phrase at different pitches), see bars 7 and 8 in the following piece; Augmentation, where the time values of each note in the melody are increased (for example doubled) and Diminution where the time values of each note are decreased; and Stretto where the subject and answer are brought closer together so that an overlap occurs. This usually happens toward the end of the piece so that tension is created before the final resolution in the last bars.

INVENTION NO XII IN A MAJOR

In this particular example, the initial melodic idea, known as the **Subject**, is stated in the Soprano Voice (Right Hand part) in the first two bars. This theme is echoed by the **Answer** which is the same melodic figure, in the Dominant key, played by the Bass voice in the Left Hand part in bars 3 and 4.

The accompanying material employed in the Left Hand part in the first two bars is then brought into the Right Hand part in bars 3 and 4 to accompany the Answer. Once the initial statement of the Subject and Answer has been completed, the remainder of the piece is concerned with 'playing' with sections of the original material in the various ways listed above.

Note also the use of 'inverted' material where the movement of each original interval is taken in the opposite direction.

For instance this figure from bar 6

occurs inverted in bar 12.

Before playing this piece, indicate the modulations and write the chord names above each bar. Mark the Cycle of Fifths progressions with a bracket. Practise the piece in Block chord forms where possible before playing the figures as written.

The music is reproduced here in an Urtext version; in other words a typeset version of the original manuscript, free of editors markings concerning dynamics, touch and phrasing. Only fingering has been added, so that you will find the study of the piece more straightforward.

You the performer, should therefore add your own ideas on phrasing touch, dynamics and tempo variations (rall or accel etc), in accordance with performances or recordings of this style of music that you have previously heard.

To play a modern piece in the style of an Invention refer to No. 3 in the Book 'Six Contemporary Pieces' by Margaret S. Brandman.

9. INVENTION No. XII

(a) Inverted Mordent - see page 84 of Book 2 of this series.

FIGURED BASS EXERCISES — SECTION 3
SECOND INVERSION CHORDS

From your harmony studies in the recommended theory books*, you should know that the Fifth degree is doubled in a Second Inversion chord. This being the case, the arrangement of the chord for piano style is a very simple matter; — just play one of each of the triad notes in the Right Hand chord. As the Left Hand is already sounding the **fifth** degree, the result will be a chord with a doubled fifth.

Below is the arrangement of a second inversion chord (a) and also a comparison of the Right Hand arrangements for the Root, First and Second inversions of the same chord (b). Notice that the right hand plays the full triad in both the Root and Second inversions while the First Inversion uses only the Root and Fifth notes.

Common places to find Second Inversion chords are: at a Cadence in the progressions I^6_4 V I or I^6_4 V vi; as passing chords in such progressions as I^6 V^6_4 I or IV I^6_4 IV^6; or as a decorative finish to a cadence, for instance V I which would be replaced by V IV^6_4 I.

After completing the Chord Table play Exercise 1.

CHORD TABLE

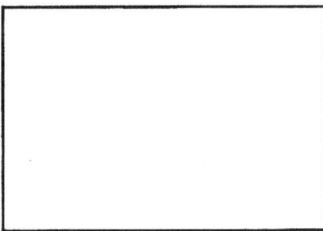

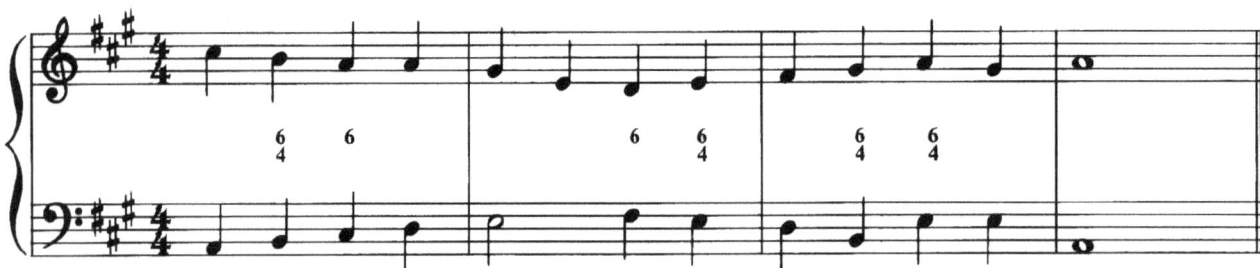

Altered Chords

If a chord has to be altered in a Figured Bass progression, from the chords which appear in the Chord Table, a Sharp, Flat or Natural sign is written before the number. If the sign appears on its own, it always refers to the note **a third away from the given bass note.**

In this way the Diminished and Augmented chords, the Neapolitan sixth chord and a chord with a Tierce de Picardie can be indicated as well as any other unusual or unexpected chords, or modulations.

Complete the Chord Table and then play Exercise 2.

CHORD TABLE

SIMPLE AND COMPOUND INTERVAL REVIEW

Simple Intervals

The intervals with a numerical value of an octave (8th) or less are known as Simple Intervals. They are as follows: Unison (Prime) 2nd, 3rd, 4th, 5th, 6th, 7th and Octave (8th).

Compound Intervals

Intervals of larger numerical value are known as 'Compound' Intervals. They are the intervals of a 9th, 10th, 11th, 12th, 13th, 14th and 15th.

The names of the notes in an interval of a 9th are the same as those in the interval of a 2nd the only difference being that the 9th is an octave further away than a 2nd.

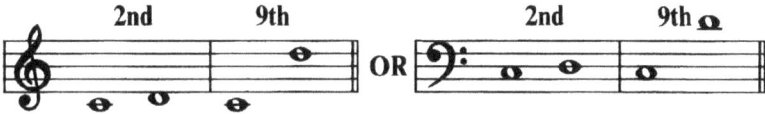

Similarly, the names of the notes in the interval of a 10th are the same as those in the interval of a 3rd; the 11th and the 4th, the 12th and the 5th and so on.

Thus the larger intervals can be named 2 ways:—

(1) as a 9th	OR	(2) as a Compound 2nd
as a 10th		as a Compound 3rd
as an 11th		as a Compound 4th
as a 12th		as a Compound 5th
as a 13th		as a Compound 6th
as a 14th		as a Compound 7th
as a 15th		as a Compound 8th

The interval qualities remain the same for both the Simple and Compound Interval.

The	**Perfect**	Intervals are:— both the Simple and Compound		1, 4, 5, 8, (11, 12, 15)
The	**Consonant** (Major+Minor)	Intervals are:— both the Simple and Compound		3 and 6 (10 and 13)
The	**Dissonant** (Major+Minor)	Intervals are:— both the Simple and Compound		2 and 7 (9 and 14)

EXTENDED CHORDS

Another theme in this section of the book is the study of extended chords — Ninths, Elevenths and Thirteenths. Below is Part One of this subject, NINTH CHORDS

EXTENDED CHORDS — PART ONE
NINTH CHORDS

The Compound Interval of a Major Ninth can be added to all the Sixth and Seventh chords discussed previously.

In Modern Chord building, unless otherwise specified*, the 9th degree is always the interval of a Major Ninth away from the Root Note.

*If the 9th is to be altered special instructions will be added to the chord name. For example: ♯9 or ♭9.

The naming of an Extended chord is governed by the type of 7th or 6th chord that is the foundation for the chord. The function of an extended chord, as a Rest chord or a Leading chord, is also still governed by the four-note foundation of the chord.

Thus if building 9th chords on the note 'C', although the four-note chord alters to suit the name, the 9th note always remains constant. (D).

e.g. Cmaj9th	=	Cmajor7th	with 'D'
C9	=	C7	with 'D'
Cm9th	=	Cm7th	with 'D'
Cdim9th	=	Cdim7th	with 'D'
C6/9	=	C6th	with 'D'
Cm6/9	=	Cm6	with 'D'
Cø9	=	Cø	with 'D'
Cm9♭5	=	Cm7♭5	with 'D'

cf. pages 1 to 21 in Contemporary Workbook 2.

Altered Chords:	Cmaj9♯5	=	Cmaj7♯5	with 'D'
	Cmaj9♭5	=	Cmaj7♭5	with 'D'
	C9♯5	=	C7♯5	with 'D'
	C9♭5	=	C7♭5	with 'D'
	Cm9♯7	=	Cm♯7	with 'D'

Example 1

Cmaj9   C9   Cm9   Cdim9   C6/9   Cm6/9

Cm9♭5   Cmaj9♯5   Cmaj9♭5   C9♯5   C9♭5   Cm9♯7

Exercise — Taking a different type of chord each day, work out all twelve of the chords as ninth chords, so that you become familiar with the sound of the chord and the keyboard shape each chord creates. For instance, on day one, play the Dominant Ninth chord either on each Root Note in the Cycle of Fifths, or moving chromatically through the octave. On day two, play all the Minor Ninth chords and so on. Vary the voicings using some of the following suggestions.

VOICING A NINTH CHORD

There are numerous ways in which to voice a Ninth Chord. Below are a few of them.

(1) Take only the Root Note in the Left Hand and play the remaining notes with the Right Hand. The upper notes can be played in any inversion above the Root Note. As long as the Left Hand is sounding the Root Note the chord is regarded as being in Root Position. The inversion changes only when the lowest note changes. See Example 2.

When playing with another instrument which is playing the Bass Line, omit the lowest note altogether and play only the upper 4 notes of the chord. These upper notes can then be played with either hand, or split between the two hands, or doubled (8 notes altogether).

Example 2   **Example 3**

(2) Play the Root and Fifth notes in the Left Hand and the remaining three notes in the Right Hand, in either open or close position, an octave or two octaves away from the Left Hand notes. See Example Three (a).

(3) Take the Root and the Seventh notes in the Left Hand and the remaining three notes in the Right Hand as before. See Example Three (b).

(4) Take the Root, 5th and 7th notes in the Left Hand and the remaining two notes in the Right Hand. See Example Four.

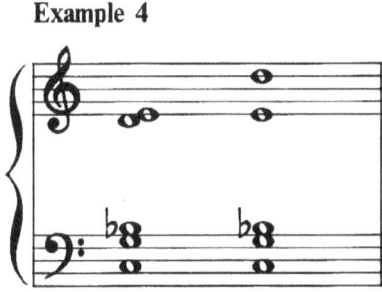

Example 4

Using INVERSIONS of a Ninth Chord. — There are many other voicing possibilities available open to the pianist using the inversions of the Ninth chords. (i.e. when any other note of the chord is played as the lowest note instead of the Root Note.) Example Five presents a few of these possibilities. Experiment with the sounds to find more for yourself.

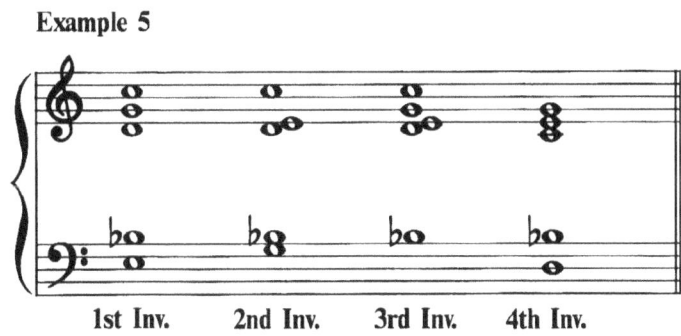

Example 5

1st Inv.   2nd Inv.   3rd Inv.   4th Inv.

ROOT PROGRESSIONS
STEP TWO

On page 16 the Chromatic Chords occuring on the Flattened Second and Flattened Sixth degrees of the scale were discussed. Further to the discussion on these chords, I would like to point out that occasionally the Italian, German and French styles of sixth chords (sounding like Dominant 7th chords) may occur on the Flattened Second degree of the scale as well as on the Flattened Sixth degree. Originally only the Neapolitan Sixth chord occurred on this degree, but these other chords are used as borrowed chords on the Flattened Second degree of the scale.

When you look closely at the German 6th form of the chord placed on the Flattened 2nd degree of the scale, (for instance D♭ German 6th in C scale), you will find that it has two notes in common with the Dominant 7th chord of the same scale. (i.e. G7 in C scale). These two notes are a distance of 3 tones apart and the interval between them is therefore commonly called a Tritone. Looking at the interval another way, it is both an Augmented 4th and a Diminished 5th interval. In both of the above-named chords the notes of the Tritone are the 3rd and 7th degrees. See Example 1a.

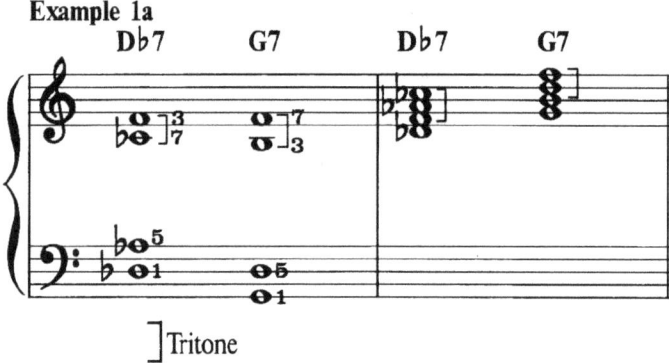

Play only these two notes and heed the strong pull of the F to the E (semitone) and the B to the C (semitone). It is the Tritone that provides the sense of pull and is the essence of any Leading Function Chord. See Example 1b.

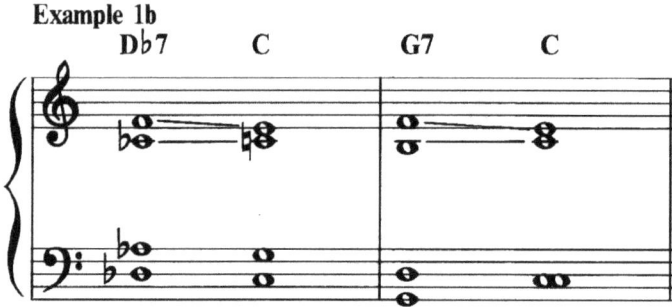

We have previously referred to the Dominant 7th (V7) and the diminished Triad on the Seventh degree (vii°) as Leading Function Chords. To these we can also add the German 6th built on the Flattened 2nd of the scale which sounds like a Dominant 7th chord (♭II7). In the jazz sense it is usually written as a Dominant Seventh chord and much more extensive use is made of the progression than ever was in classical music.

The chord on the Flattened Second usually resolves directly onto the Tonic chord. See Example 1c.

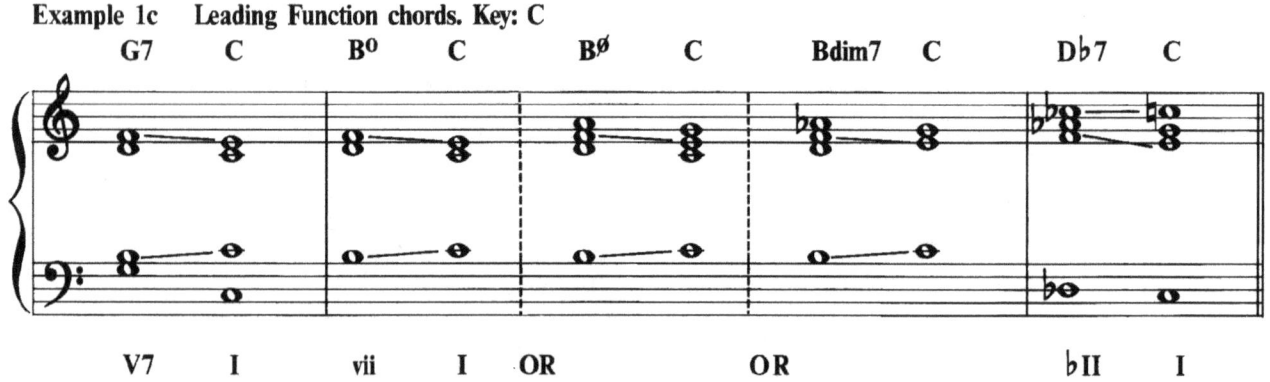

The second stage in the series on Root Progressions, is based on the principle demonstrated in the first section of the discussion; that is: that the V7 chord can be replaced by the chord on the Flattened Second degree of the scale.

Using the twelve-bar blues progression of Step I as a starting point (cf p 33) replace the V7th chords found in the boxed positions with the Dominant Seventh built on the Flattened 2nd (♭II) degree of the scale of the goal chord. (i.e. A German 6th chord). The Root Progression at this point will be by descending semitones. See Example 2 Bars 4 to 5.

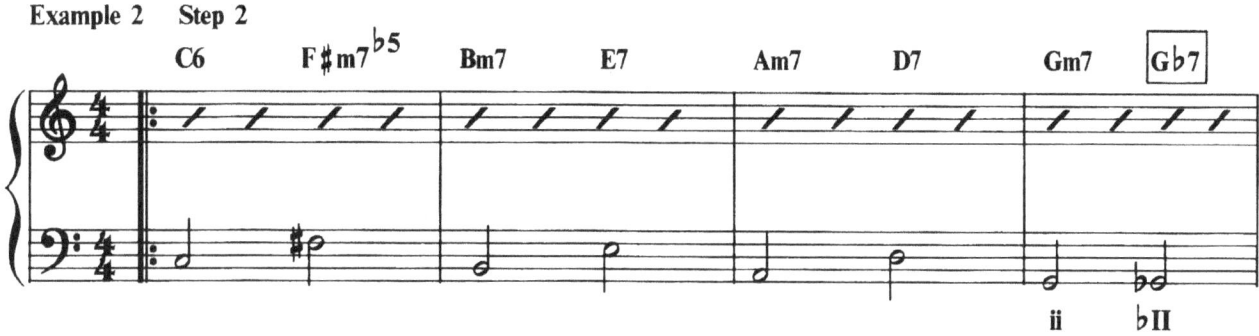

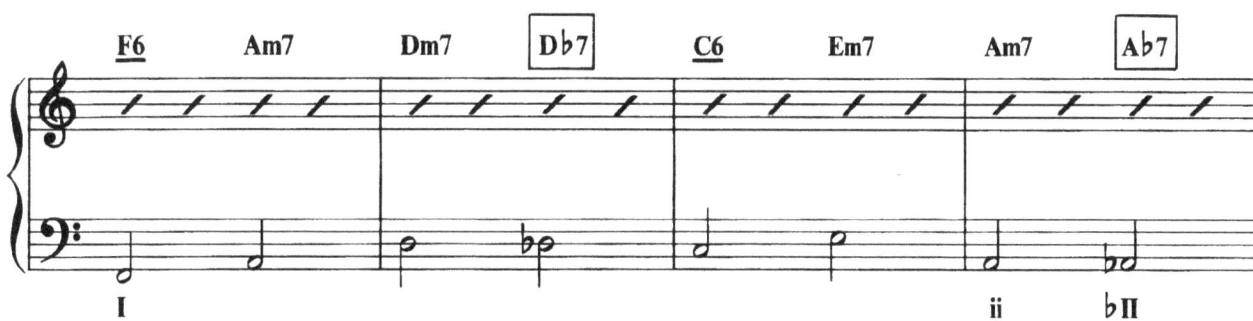

Compare each of the ♭II7ths in Example 2 to the original Dominant 7th in the box and you will find only two altered notes. The Tritone (3rd—7th) remains constant.

N.B. Another connection between these two chords is found in the Dominant 7th chord with a Flattened 5th. You will find that G7♭5 in its second inversion is exactly the same as D♭7♭5. (This is also the French 6th sound). Try using this altered form of the Dominant 7th as an alternative to the straight Dominant 7th, in some tunes. See Example 3.

Example 3

G7♭5　C　　D♭7♭5　C　　D♭7♭5　C　　G7♭5　C

* = written enharmonically

Thus in many melodies the V7 leading to I can be replaced by the ♭II7 leading to I providing that it suits the melody. It is a very subtle and smooth jazz sound. Make sure it is appropriate for the tune you are playing. It really would not suit many simple rock tunes and the like!

Often the quality of this chord can be changed to a minor 7th or Major 7th chord or 9ths and 13ths are added to the basic chord. Experiment to hear what sounds best in each individual tune.

Play the Blues progression (Example Two) adding 9ths to the four-note chords indicated.

Good examples of the II-♭II-I progression can be found in the Bossa-Nova songs of Antonio Carlos Jobim, especially 'Girl from Ipanema' and Quiet Nights of Quiet Stars (Corcovado).

Use the Manuscript below to devise your own chord progressions.

10. EVANESCENCE

This piece makes use of several of the chord structures and progressions mentioned thus far in this book.

The opening bars use snippets of the **Cycle of Fifths** progressions that were discussed in STEP ONE of the topic of Root Progressions.

In bar 8 there is an example of a Flattened Second substitute chord being used. (cf. STEP TWO of Root Progressions). In this case the D Flat chord is used instead of (substituted for) the dominant 7th chord, G7.

Fill in the bar numbers in which the Flattened Second substitute chord is used. Bar 8., Bar .... and Bar ....

Ninth Chords

The various types of Ninth Chords have been freely used in this piece. Some chords use further extensions (11ths etc.) while others incorporate some of the altered chord notes discussed earlier in this book.

For more information on the altered notes in the upper extension notes of the chords, refer to either Book Two of the Contemporary Chord Workbook series or Book Four of this piano method.

Accents

The accents used in this piece are used in the Jazz sense.

>   means a long, heavy accent. Usually found on a main beat or anticipation of a main beat.

∧ or ∨   means a short sharp accent. Usually found on the weaker beats or pulses. Used to enhance the syncopated effect.

Swing Feel

As the piece is in Swing Feel (Jazz Timing), the count will be 1+a 2+a 3+a 4+a.

Two straight quavers ♫ become an uneven triplet ♩₃♪.

See page 80 of Book 2A in this series for more detail.

Notice the use of the syncopated chordal accompaniment to the melody. Thus the feel of the piece is dependant upon the triplet count, the syncopation and accents and on the implied stress on the second quaver in each pair. Place any semiquavers written thus ♩♬ on the last third of the triplet.

e.g.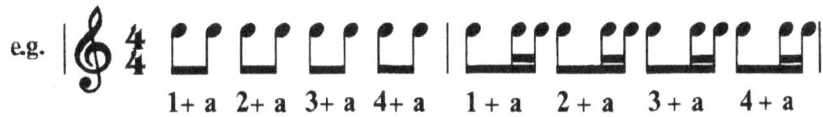

EXTENDED CHORDS — PART TWO
ELEVENTHS

The interval of a Perfect Eleventh (Compound 4th) can be added to a Ninth chord to form an Eleventh chord. As mentioned, on page 42, extended chords function according to the four-note foundation of the chord. That is if the foundation notes of the chord are a Dominant 7th, the extended versions of the chord will also act as Dominant chords.

The Perfect Eleventh interval is usually added to only four of the 9th chords mentioned earlier. These chords are: the Major 9th, Dominant 9th, Minor 9th, and Minor 9th Flattened 5th chords. They become the Major 11th, Dominant 11th, Minor 11th and Minor 11th Flattened 5th respectively.

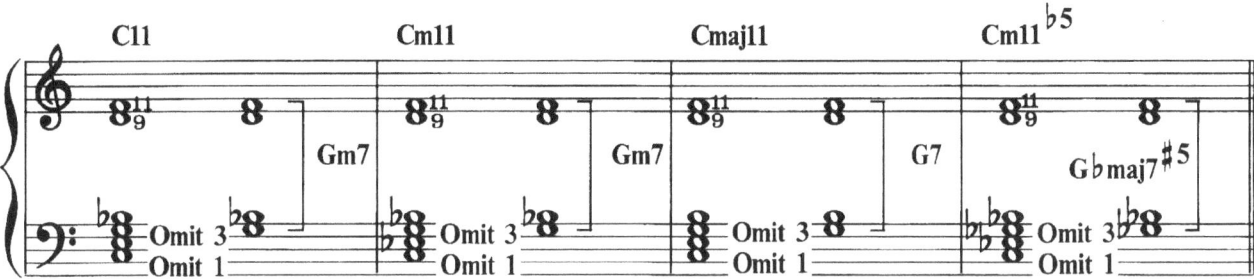

These chords are very full sounding chords owing to the larger number of notes. As such, they also become impossible to play with one hand.

To solve these problems, certain notes can be omitted to make the chord easier to handle, or less clustered, while still preserving the essential sound of the chord. The omitted notes are the 3rd, (too close to the Compound 4th) and the Root Note, (too close to the Compound 2nd). The remaining four notes of each Eleventh chord can be seen as a type of Seventh chord placed over a Bass Note a Fifth lower.

Thus, C11 = Gm7/C.

In the same manner Cmaj11 can be written G7/C and Cm11♭5 can be written G♭maj7♯5/C.
(See Book Four Polychords).

The pianist can play the 11th sound in the Left Hand as an accompaniment, by pedalling the low Bass Note and connecting it to the remaining notes, played in the middle register of the keyboard. If the pianist is fulfilling the function of accompanist to a singer or instrumentalist, then the chord could be split between the Left and Right Hands, in the above manner, without the use of the pedal.

However, if playing with a Bass player, the pianist can leave out the Root Note altogether, play the four-note version of the chord in the Left Hand, and supply a Melody Line with the Right Hand.

Work out the four types of Elevenths listed on this page on all twelve semitones of the octave.

Apply the suggestions given for voicing the 9th chords, on page 41 to the Eleventh chords given in Example 1.

ROOT PROGRESSIONS
STEP THREE

On page 44 the relationship between the Seventh chords built on the Dominant (V7) and Flattened Second (♭II7) degrees of the scale was discussed.

The common notes between the two chords being the 3rd and 7th degrees of each chord, which are the distance of a TRITONE apart.

When you observe the Diminished Triad found on the Seventh degree of the scale, you will notice that it too, has the same 2 notes.

In the Key of C these chords would be: V7 — G7 (G.B.D.F), ♭II7 — D♭7 (D♭.F.A♭.C♭) and vii⁰ — Bdim (B.D.F). See Example 1.

The diminished triad can be used with a seventh added to it. In a Major Key the chord thus formed becomes a Half-Diminished 7th (Minor 7♭5) chord. In the minor key it becomes a Diminished Seventh chord. See Example 2.

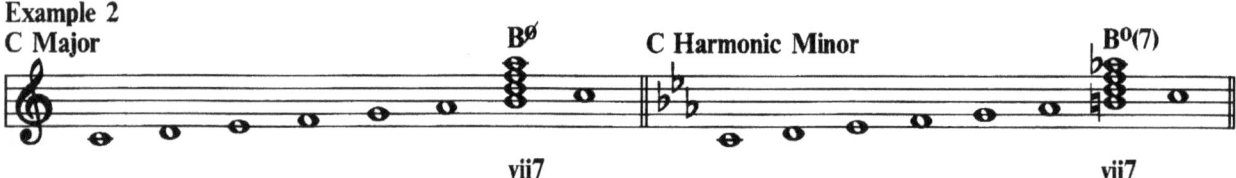

You can use the Diminished Seventh chord as a SUBSTITUTE for the Dominant Seventh (V7) chord, in the boxed positions in the 12-Bar Blues pattern. As the Blues is a Major Blues, you can also use the Half-Diminished 7th chord in the same places. Only the Full Diminished 7th chord is suitable for a Minor Key. cf p.32. Contemporary Chord Workbook. Book 1.

The Root Progression now moves by a rising semitone. (In Step II, it moved by a falling semitone, and in Step I by falling fifths.)

Play the Blues given below and mix and match the types of chords in the BOXED positions. You have the choice of V7, ♭II7 and vii Diminished Triad, Half-Diminished 7th and Full Diminished 7th in each case.

I feel that the use of too many Diminished 7th chords is a little over-powering, even too classical. Find a pleasant mixture of the above chords to add colour and variety to your substitute progression.

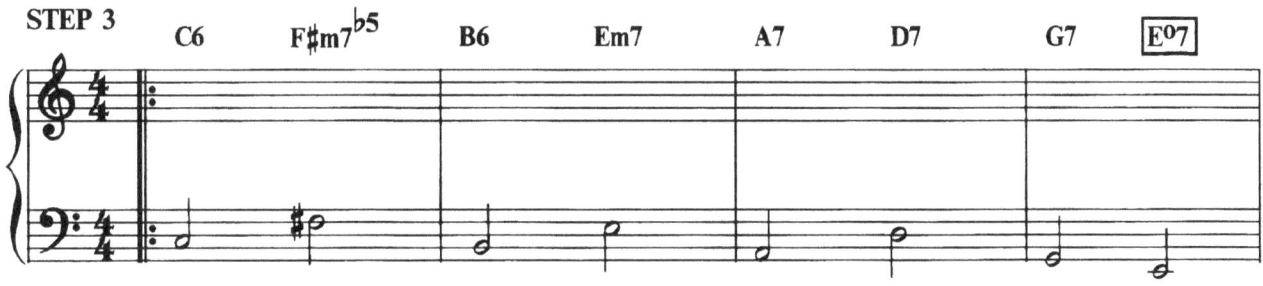

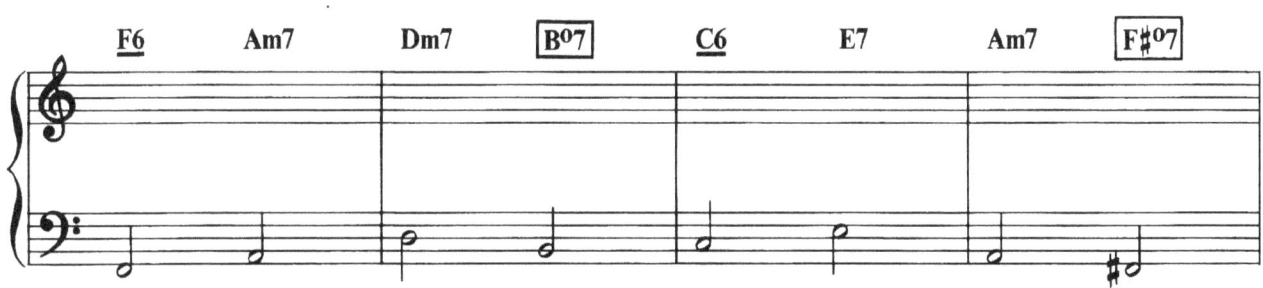

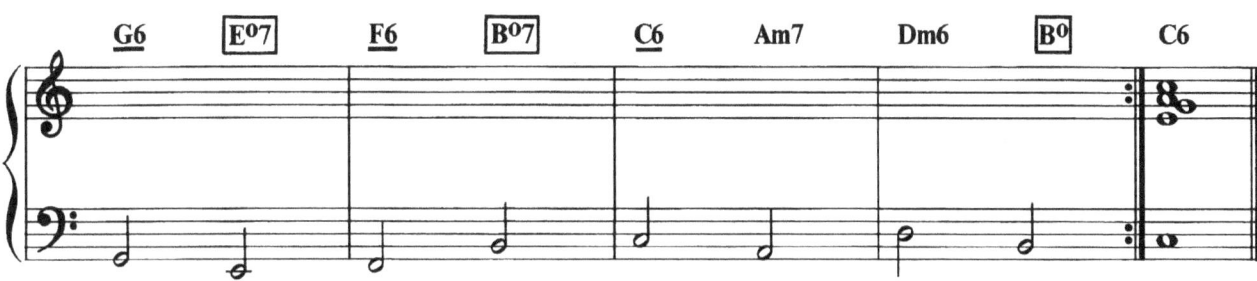

☐ Use either V7, ♭II7 or vii°, viiø, vii°7 in the boxed positions.
  Play the above progression extending the chords to Ninths and Elevenths.

THE MODAL SEVENTH SUBSTITUTE CHORD

There is another commonly found Dominant substitute chord, used by many Jazz players. The Root Note of the chord is the Flattened Seventh degree of the scale, and the resolution of the chord is upwards by a whole-step. This fact gives the progression the Modal sound. If you look ahead to page 77 you will see that the Dorian, Phrygian, Mixolydian, Aeolian and Locrian modes all have whole-steps between the 7th and 8th degrees whereas in Major and Harmonic Minor scales the distance between the 7th and 8th degrees is a half-step.

In the key of 'C' the progression in question would move from B♭7 to C. Once again the reason for the success of the progression lies in the fact that the TRITONE (D to A♭) is found in the B♭7 chord. The progression sounds even better when the Dominant Ninth chord is used instead of the Dominant Seventh. Often the B♭7 chord is approached by a chord on the Flattened 6th of the scale (A♭) so that the entire progression can be seen as moving along the notes of the Natural Minor scale (Aeolian Mode).

Another common place to find the Modal seventh substitute chord is in the place of the **minor iv chord** in the progression IV (Major) to iv (minor) to I (Major), where by simply adding a bass note a Perfect Fifth below the original chord a Dominant Ninth chord is created on the Flattened Seventh degree.

For example: F Fm C becomes F Fmi/B♭ Bass C which is equivalent to F B♭9 C.

Play this example.

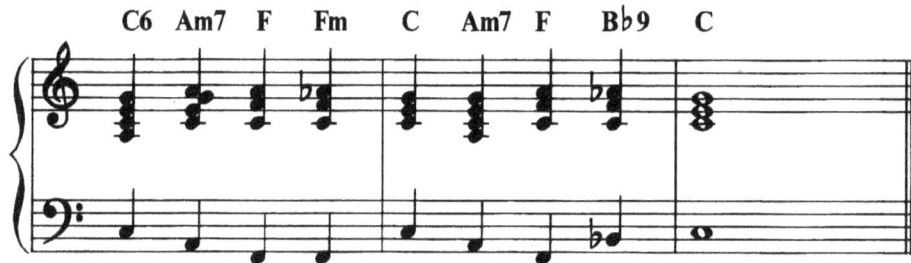

Use the manuscript below to devise your own chord progressions.

TWO-PART INVENTION No. XIII by J. S. BACH

This invention is an interesting example of Invention technique, as it displays many sequences and imitations. As well there are some cycle progressions and uses of the vii7 (diminished and half-diminished seventh chords) as a substitute chord in the cycle progression c.f. Step Three of the series on Root Progressions.

Before playing this piece, analyse the chords and modulations and indicate them on the music. Practise the Broken chord figures first as **Block Chord** units, then split them up as the written figure indicates. Be sure to note whether the chord is a three, four or five-note chord shape. No doubt you will remark on the use of Major and Minor 7th chords which are generally not expected in 'Classical' music!

Once again this piece has been reproduced in an Urtext version. You will therefore need to add your own ideas on touch, phrasing dynamics and tempo variations.

Here are three suggestions for phrasing and touch for the first two bars. Select one of these, or decide on a style of your own and then follow the ideas through on any similar musical figures for the duration of the piece.

12. INVENTION No. XIII

J. S. Bach

I would strongly urge the keen musician to explore the complete set of two-part inventions by J.S. Bach, once the examples presented in this book have been learnt.

APPLYING STEPS I, II, III ROOT PROGRESSION SUBSTITUTIONS

Below are some suggestions on how to use Leading Function chords (Steps I, II, III) as substitute chords.

In the example below, there are only two chords used in bars 20 and 21. Working backwards from the goal chord, the B flat chord at the beginning of section B, we could use four chords lasting two beats each to replace the existing chords.

13. SEASONS OF LOVE
Margaret Brandman

Write your own lyrics for this song

Here is a suggestion for the first line:
Spring and summer are the times for love
When the sun is shining up above....

CHORD TABLE

IV	I	V
Eb	Bb	F7
ii	vi	iii
Cm	Gm	Dm
		vii°
		A°

Using Step I, the Root Notes of D, G, C, F, will lead to the goal chord B♭. If you refer to your CHORD TABLE for B♭, this will tell you which chord qualities (Major, Minor, Diminished etc.) to place above the Root Notes. See Example 2.

STEP 1

If you want to alter the chord qualities from those in the Chord Table, (which implies a modulation), try various types of chord qualities to see which of them you think best suits the melody. (Try Major, Minor and Dominant 7th, Minor 7♭5 chords and Major and Minor 6th chords.) Make sure that the altered chord does not clash with the melody note, unless you particularly want the clashy sound. See Example 3.

Example 3   STEP 1   Variations

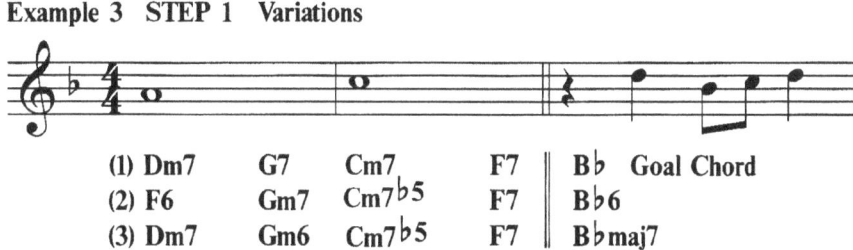

To use Step II, make sure that you have completed Step 1 correctly then replace (substitute) one or two chords in the progression with chords built on the Flattened 2nd degree of the goal chord or chords. Next try various types of 6ths and 7ths above the Root Note finding the one which best suits the melody according to your taste. See Example 4.

Example 4   STEP 2

To use Step III, follow the same procedure as for Step II and replace one or two chords with the chord built on the 7th degree of the goal chord scale. (Either Diminished 7th or Half-Diminished 7th [mi7♭5]). See Example 5.

Example 5   STEP 3

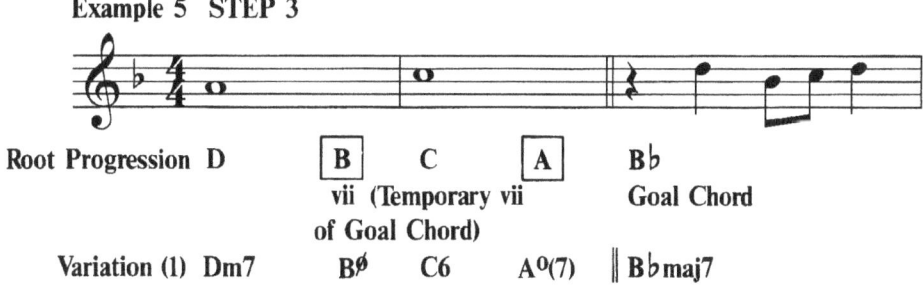

Now apply the same procedure to bars 25 through 28, using one chord per bar, and to bars 3 and 4 using two chords per bar. To complete the exercise, find suitable extension chords for each given chord and any other substitute chords that could be used to replace the existing chord sequence. Keep in mind that most Dominant chords can be replaced by a II7 V7 progression, giving each chord half of the time value of the original chord symbol. e.g. A bar of C7 will become half a bar of Gm7 followed by half a bar of C7.

TURN-AROUNDS. The procedure of applying substitute chords that has been discussed above is frequently used in the last 2 bars of an eight-bar phrase in order to provide a smooth link with the next phrase. The use of two chords per bar for bars 7 and 8 usually contrasts with the earlier part of the phrase which for the most part would have one chord per bar. The faster chord movement provides impetus and tension which is released as the tune settles in to the next eight-bar phrase. The number of chords per bar indicates the Harmonic Rhythm of the tune.

This linking procedure is known as a Turn-Around. Many jazz tutors list them but do not give instructions on how to find or invent a Turn-Around for yourself. There are a great number of variations of the Turn-Around, but if you follow the method outlined here, using the Root Progression as a basis, you can create Turn-Arounds at the drop of a hat without having to consult the manual.

To make up an introduction (intro) to a tune use the same procedure. A four bar intro could be four bars of one chord per bar or a two bar progression, using two chords per bar, played TWICE.

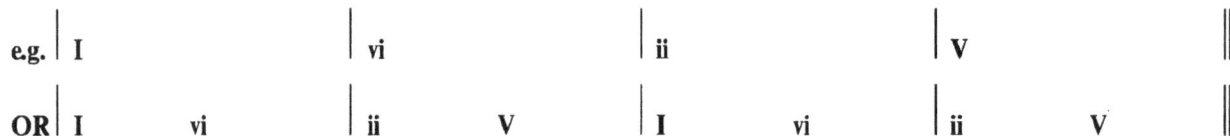

e.g. | I | vi | ii | V ||

OR | I   vi | ii   V | I   vi | ii   V ||

The other Root Progressions covered in this book can also be used as vehicles for devising **Turn-Arounds, Introductions,** and **Substitute Chord Progressions**.

HANDY MANUSCRIPT

FOUR-NOTE ARPEGGIO FINGERINGS

The fingerings for four-note arpeggios are in many ways simpler to find, than those for the three-note arpeggios. As all five fingers are being used the choice is narrowed down. Once again the rule of starting white-note arpeggios with the R.H. thumb and L.H. 5th finger applies. This also applies to any inversion that begins on a white note.

For those arpeggios which begin on a black note, the rule of placing the R.H. thumb on the first white note ascending and the L.H. thumb on the first white note descending, applies.

When this position has been found, once again, stretch the hand to the octave above and see which fingers fit comfortably onto the other notes. In a substantially white note arpeggio such as C7 Root Position, therefore, the Right Hand would use the fingers 1 2 3 4 1 2 3 4 5 over two octaves. Similarly the Left Hand would use 5 4 3 2 1 4 3 2 1. The same fingering could also be used for the first and second inversions, starting on the appropriate notes.

In some pieces it may be more convenient to begin the first inversion on the second finger (R.H.) In other words applying the Root Position fingering to all inversions. However, I recommend that the arpeggios be practised in all the varied hand shapes that are created by the application of the above rules.

See Example 1 for a selection of arpeggios and the way that they can be fingered.

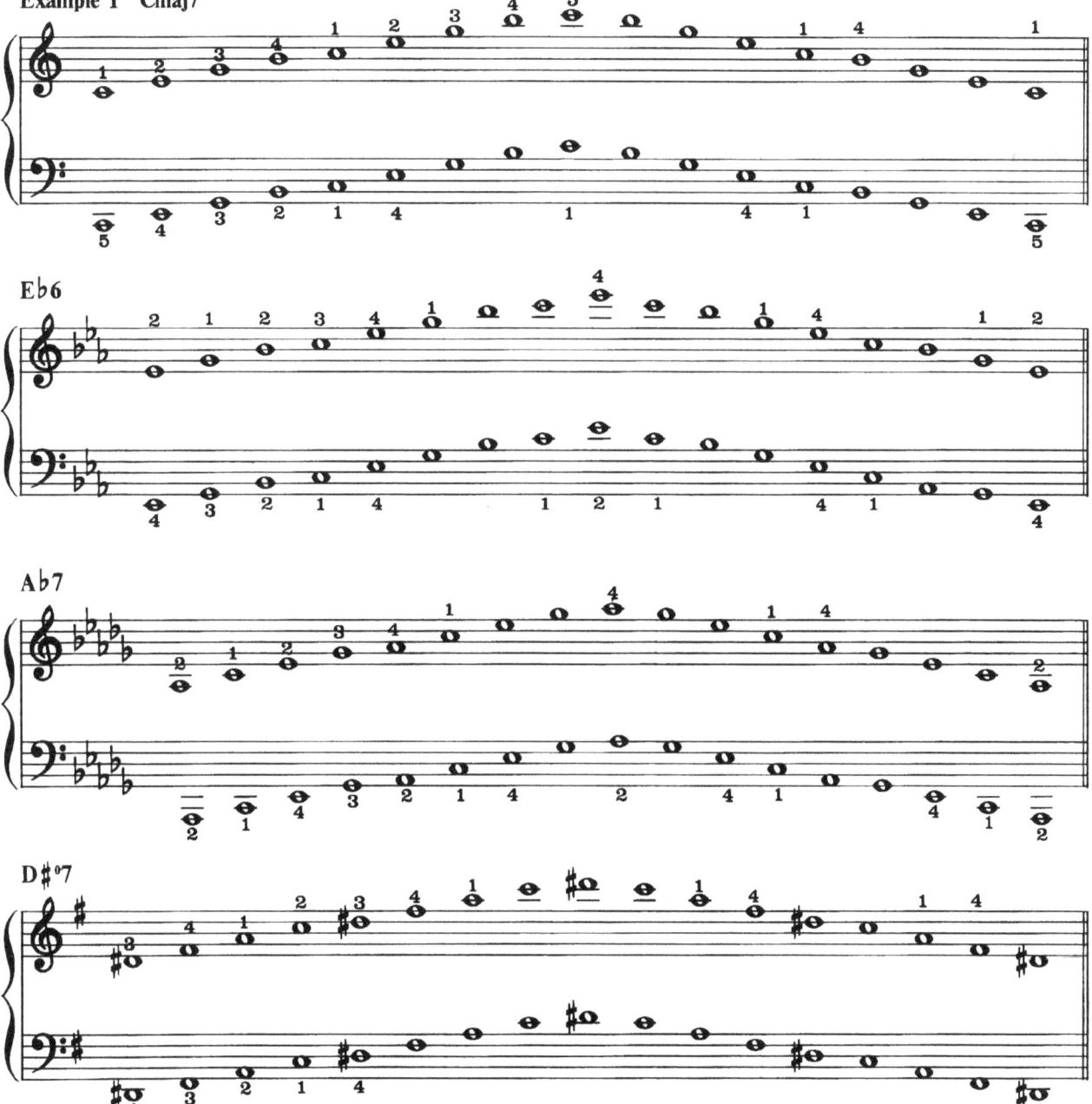

RONDO FORM

The basic concept behind the Rondo form is that of a circular or 'rounded' form. The first section, which is usually labelled 'A' and is in the Tonic Key, returns after each 'Episode' or excursion. The Episodes, each one different to the other, are usually in the Dominant or Relative Major or Minor to the original key, or at least in a closely related key as can be found on the chord table. These sections are labelled 'B' and 'C' respectively.

Thus the form of a Rondo can be expressed as A B A C A. Often there is a short Coda (or tailpiece) after the last A section. This is used to provide a more satisfying finish to the piece. There may be also extended Rondo forms with more contrasting sections added.

The following piece is in basic Rondo form. Analyse the form and note the keys of the B and C sections. Write the chords in above each bar so that you can understand the Root Progressions used.

The second last chord of the piece is an altered ninth chord. Refer to the section in Book Four on the subject or see page 41 of the Contemporary Chord Workbook, Book 2.

SONATA FORM

The following is a brief description of the Sonata form of the Classical period. As even the First Movement of a Sonata is usually four to five pages long, I have not included one in this book. However I strongly urge the student to refer to a book of Sonatas by either Haydn, Mozart or Beethoven to play and analyse.

When Sonata form is referred to it can be understood from two points of view. Firstly, the term Sonata Form is used to describe an entire Sonata: that is —

First Movement	— usually lively and in 'First Movement Sonata' form.
Second Movement	— usually Slow and in either ABA, Sonata or Variation form.
Third Movement	— either a Minuet and Trio or a Scherzo and Trio (this movement is optional)
Fourth Movement	— lively and in Rondo or Sonata Form.

Secondly, distinct from the entire Sonata is the 'First Movement Sonata' form, which as seen above could also be applied to other movements.

Here is a brief resumé of the 'First Movement Sonata Form' which is broadly divided into three sections:—

EXPOSITION
    First Subject — Tonic Key — usually lively
    Bridge passage — a modulatory transition
    Second Subject — Dominant Key (or Relative Major when the Tonic key is Minor) — usually more lyrical,
    Codetta — closing section. Dominant key mostly.

DEVELOPMENT
    Free use of First and Second subject materials, plus additional materials if necessary. Usually contains frequent modulations.

RECAPITULATION
    (recapping). This is a restatement of the original subjects in other keys.
    First Subject — in either Tonic or Subdominant Keys
    Bridge passage
    Second Subject — in Tonic Key
    Codetta — Tonic Key
    Optional Coda. This section which is usually faster, can vary from a brief section to a quite lengthy section and is used to increase dramatic tension. It is also usually in the Subdominant or Tonic key, finishing of course in the Tonic Key.

This form is used for both instrumental Sonatas and Symphonies. Listen to the First Movements of such Symphonies as Mozart's Symphony No. 40 in G minor or Dvorak's 'New World' Symphony, in E minor (No. 9 Op 95).

There are many other musical forms employed in composition, some of which were discussed in Book 2 of this series. Other forms are the Theme and Variation form, (refer to Sunshowers on the River in the Book Six Contemporary Piano Pieces by myself) and the Dance forms, Allemande, Courante etc.

To help you in your study of Musical Form, I would strongly recommend Dulcie Holland's tape course 'Musical Form Explained' published by Modern Music Craft.

CHORD TABLE   **CHORD TABLE**   **CHORD TABLE**

14. MANDALA SONG

Andante

Margaret S. Brandman

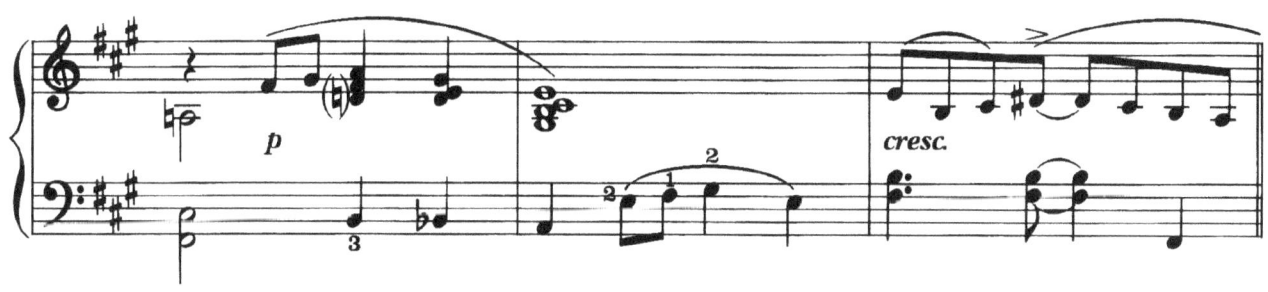

64

*Dominant 7th♯9. See Book Four.

EXTENDED CHORDS — PART THREE
THIRTEENTHS

The interval of a Major Thirteenth (Compound 6th) can be added to an Eleventh chord to form a Thirteenth chord.

The thirteenth degree is usually only added to two unaltered chords. These chords are (1) the Dominant 11th chord and (2) the Minor 11th chord. The better sounding of the two chords is the Minor 13th chord, as there is no clash between the 3rd of the chord and the 11th (Comp. 4th) degree. However, generally the rule of omitting the 3rd when the 11th is present can be applied, the result being that the notes actually played for both chords are the same.

It is possible to add the 13th degree to the Major 11th and Min 11♭5 chords but owing to the clash sound of the upper extension notes with the four foundation notes of each chord, these chords are used much less frequently than the Dom 13th and Min 13th chords. They are more likely to be found in the music of Contemporary Serious Composers than in Popular and Jazz tunes.

The Major 13th is found on the Tonic degree of the Major scale and a Minor 13♭5, is built by adding the interval of a Major 13th (Comp. Maj6) to the Minor 11♭5 chord.

Example 1a shows the full Thirteenth chords mentioned above, and Example 1b shows the same chords in their four-note form with the appropriate notes omitted. In this example the chords can be named in two ways.

Example 1a

Example 1b

*No difference as 3rd & 5th degrees are omitted.

Play these four types of Thirteenth chords on all 12 semitones of the octave. Vary the voicings, applying the voicing suggestions given for Ninth chords on page 43 to the 13th chords.

Practise also resolving the Dominant 13th chord to an extended Tonic chord for instance the Major 9th chord or the Major 6/9th chord or the Minor 9th chord.

For Example

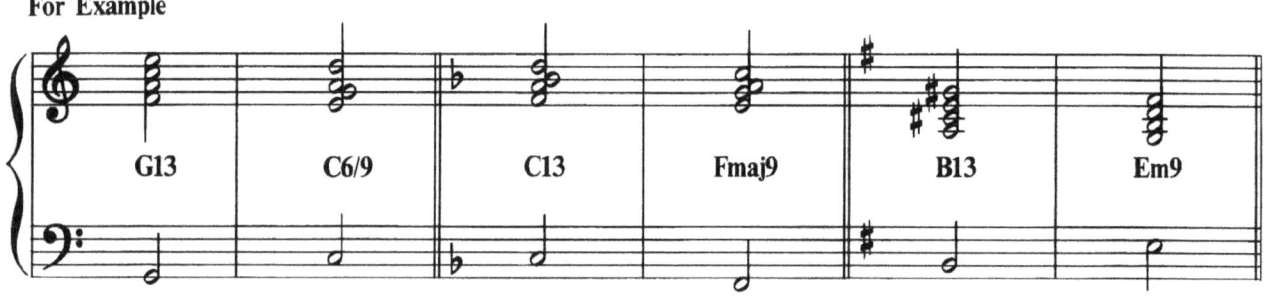

15. POLONAISE from FRENCH SUITE No. VI

J. S. Bach
Arr. for C Clef by M.S. Brandman

16. SHENANDOAH

The following piece is an arrangement of a traditional American folk-tune — Shenandoah. The arrangement presents four variations of the tune which is itself a Pentatonic melody.

Analyse the chords taking particular note of the thirteenth chords and the types of Root Progressions used. Have a close look at the treatment of the melody in the four sections and complete the questions below.

How are the melody and accompaniment treated in:

Section 1? ....

....

Section 2? ....

....

Section 3? ....

....

Section 4? ....

....

FOUR AGAINST THREE

In book 2B of this series there was a section dealing with the ways in which to play and count units of 2 against 3, on page 167.

In the third section of this piece there are several situations where an eighth note triplet is played against four sixteenth notes. In order to understand how to count and feel 'four against three', the common denominator of both units must be found.

This common denominator is the number **twelve**. The easiest way to see the connection is to divide twelve sixteenth notes (semiquavers) by both four and three so that the placement of each of the beats can be found.

When counting FOUR against THREE, in other words when you wish to see the unit basically in terms of three (counting three numbers), the unit can be viewed in this manner:

Example 1

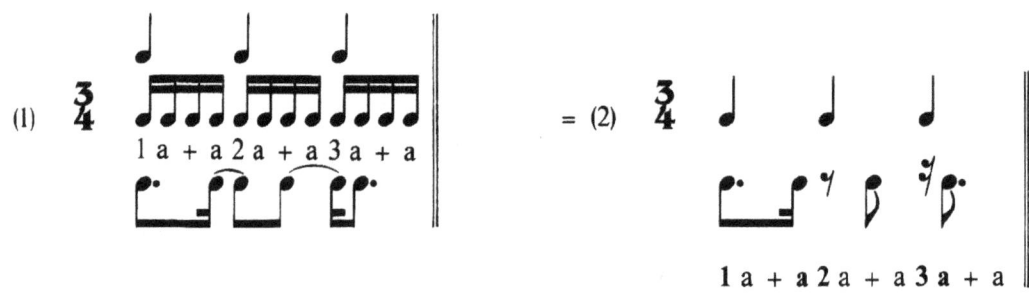

When written as a combined rhythm on one line it becomes:

When counting THREE against FOUR, in other words when you wish to see the unit basically in terms of four (counting four numbers), the unit can be viewed in this manner:

Example 2

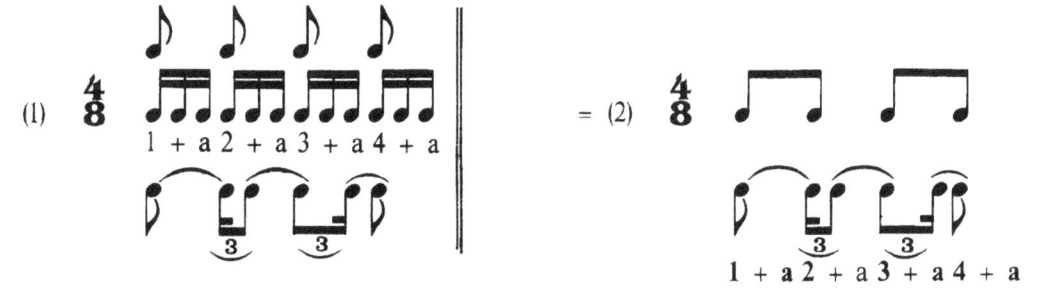

When written as a combined rhythm on one line it becomes:

Clap the rhythms in both Examples 1 and 2, so that you become comfortable with the combined sound of three against four, or four against three. Then when you see the rhythm notated for smaller note values, as in the following piece, you will know how the unit should sound and fit together, without necessarily having to count it out.

If you are still having trouble, then you should slow the tempo down and go back to counting the unit out in the ways described above.

SHENANDOAH

Traditional

O, Shenandoah, I long to see you,
Far-way you rolling river;
O, Shenandoah, I long to see you,
Away, I'm bound away,
'Cross the wide Missouri.

O, Shenandoah, I'm bound to leave you,
Far-away you rolling river;
O, Shenandoah I'll not deceive you,
Away, I'm bound away,
'Cross the wide Missouri.

FIGURED BASS EXERCISES — SECTION 4
SEVENTH CHORDS IN ROOT POSITION AND FIRST INVERSION

The figuring for Seventh chords in all inversions is as follows: (a) the full figuring with the numbers that are understood in brackets and (b) the standard figuring with the numbers that are understood being omitted.

	Root Position	First Inversion	Second Inversion	Third Inversion
(a)	7	6	(6)	(6)
	(5)	5	4	4
	(3)	(3)	3	2
(b)	7	6	4	4
		5	3	2

As you can see from the above figuring chart, the standard figuring for a Seventh chord is simply the number 7. This could apply to any of the scale-tone chords, resulting in Tonic Sevenths, Supertonic Sevenths, Mediant Sevenths and so on. To play a seventh chord in Root Position, take the Root Note in the Bass and the remaining 3 notes in the Right Hand.

When a 7 appears, build the chord according to the scale and the chord table. It is a good idea to name each chord above the music as a Major Seventh (Maj7) Minor Seventh (mi7) or Dominant Seventh (7) etc, and to indicate the degree number below the bass notes as shown in Bar 1 of Exercise 1.

The figuring for the First Inversion Seventh chord is $^6_5$. For those players who are familiar with the terminology and workings of Modern chords and their symbols (as all students that have worked through this series should be) the first inversion 7th chords can in many cases be thought of as the 'chord of the added sixth', that is, the Major and Minor Sixth chords. Other times the chord will have the same overall shape as a sixth chord but can be named only according to its original seventh shape.

After completing the chord tables play the following exercises.

CHORD TABLE

CHORD TABLE

Exercise 1

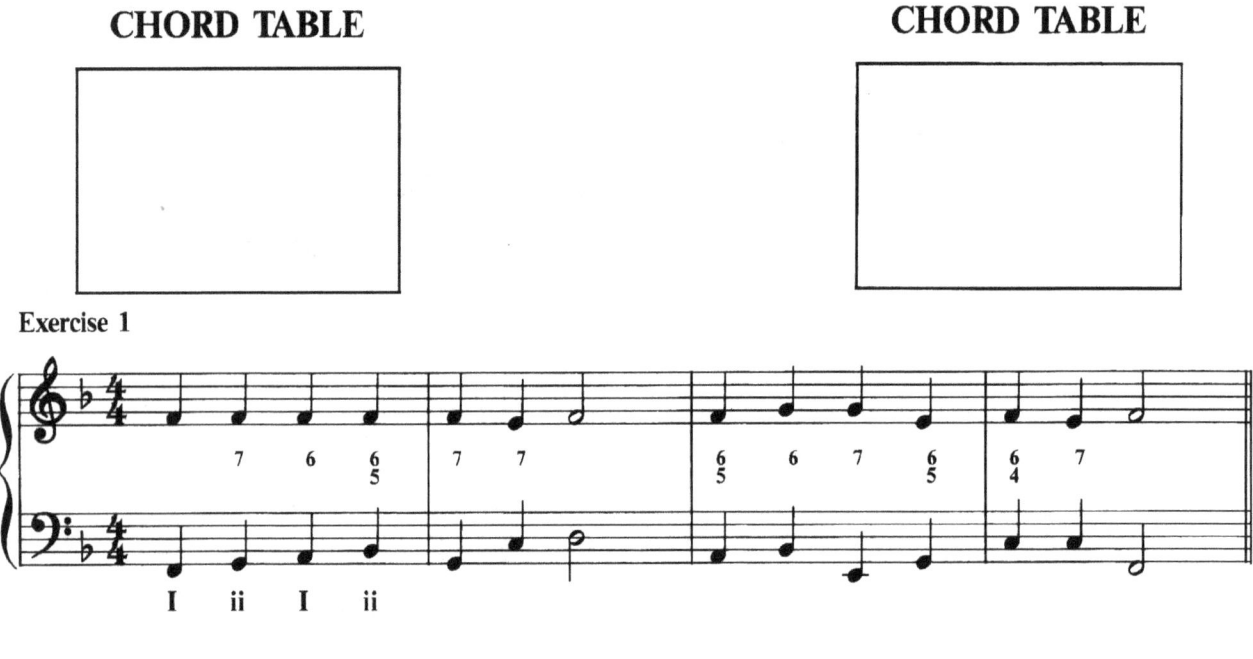

Exercise 2

THE DEVELOPMENT OF MODES
1. EARLY GREEK MODES

The information we have on the early Greek Modes dates from the Greek Mathematician Pythagoras in the Sixth Century B.C., and from various works written by other Mathematicians and theorists.

The Modes are based on a TETRACHORD (a four-note group). The outer tones of a Tetrachord were a Perfect Fourth apart and the inner tones were variably spaced with tones, semitones or quarter tones. In the Diatonic type, the notes were spaced (counting down from the top note) by a Tone, Tone and Semitone.

Two Tetrachords could then be placed either next to one another, or so that the last note of one overlapped with the first note of the next, thus creating either 7 or 8 scales.

The naming of these Modes was based on regions and tribes in ancient Greece: Lydia, Doria, Phrygia and so on.

As to the style and usage of the music of the period, very few examples of any written nature have survived the ages, so there is no real way for us to hear what the music sounded like.

The Eight TONOI or MODES

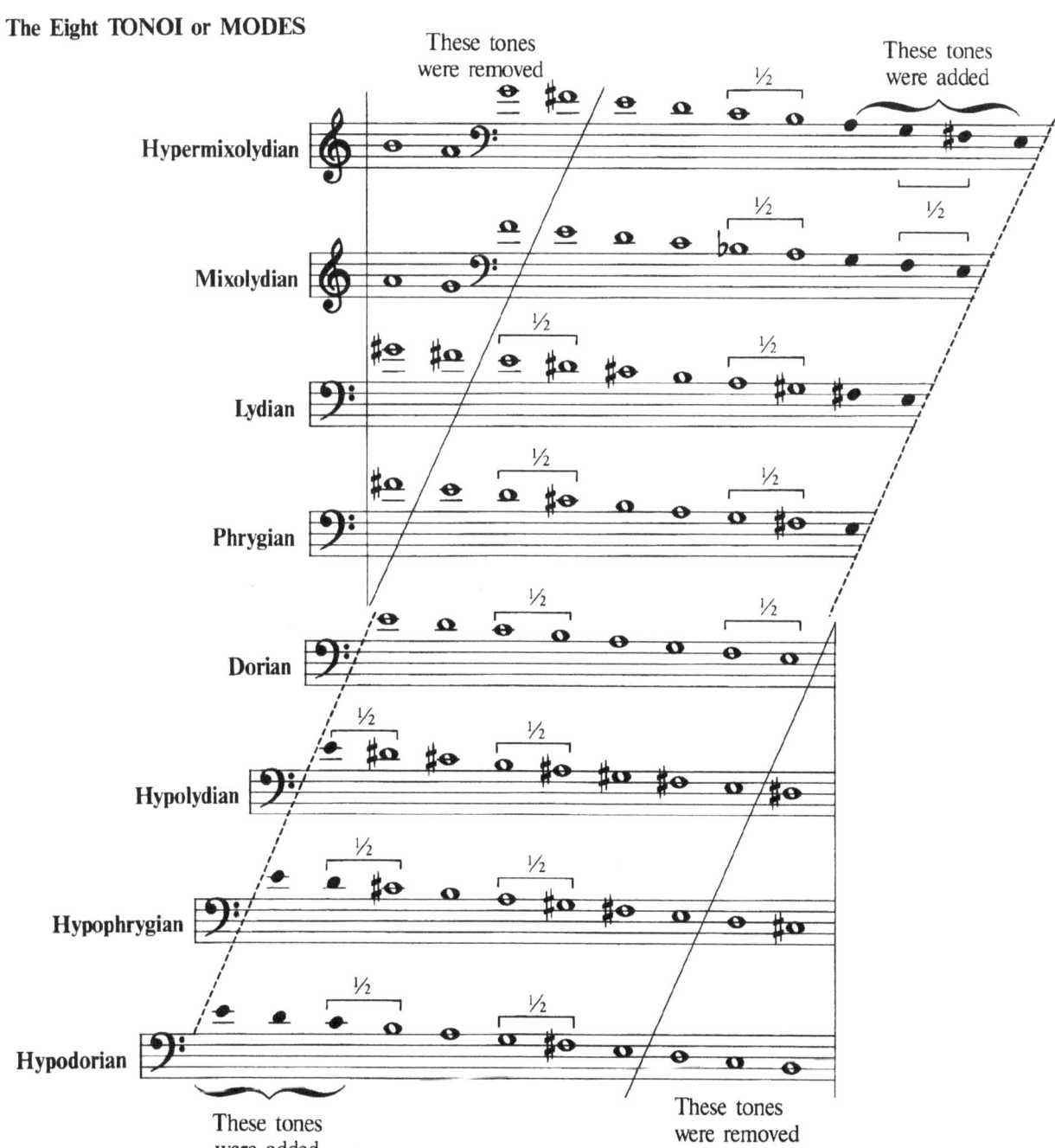

2. EARLY CHURCH MODES AND PLAINCHANT

Over a period of several centuries, the Plainchant of the Roman Church took shape. The modal system of the time achieved its complete form by the Eleventh Century A.D. The Modes became known as 'Gregorian Modes' after the Roman Catholic 'Pope Gregory' who was responsible for the organisation and collection of Church Music in the Sixth Century A.D. After many centuries of being handed down in the aural tradition, a form of notation was devised so that we now have records of what the Modes were.

At this time, there were eight modes each one octave in range, which could be distinguished by the different arrangement of tones and semitones in each one. Each Mode had a *Finalis* or Final, which was usually the last note in the melody, and a *Dominant*, also known as *Reciting Tone* or *Tenor* which sometimes functioned as a secondary tonal centre.

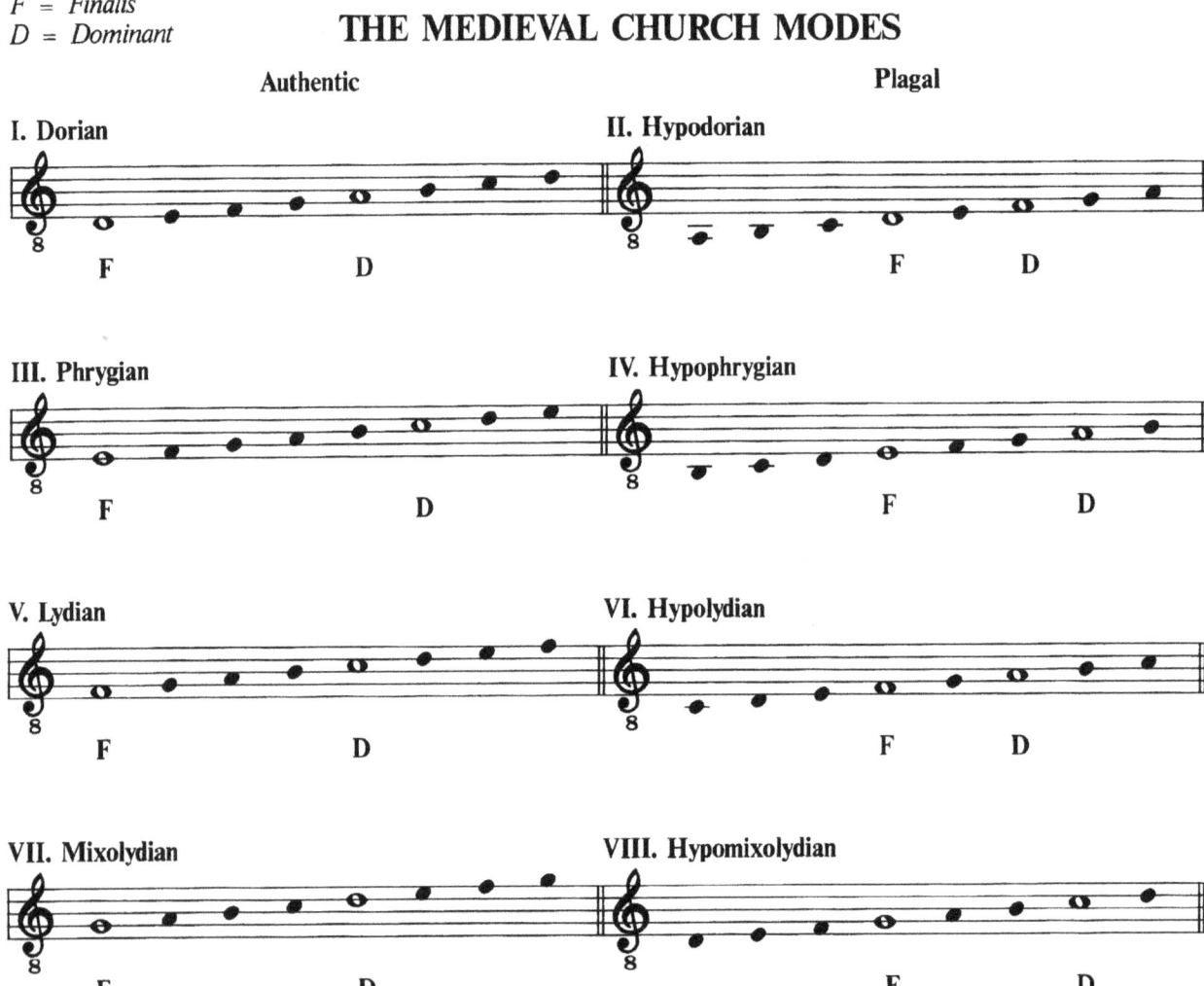

'The Modes were identified by numbers, and grouped in pairs; the odd-numbered modes were called *authentic* ('original'), and the even numbered modes *plagal* ('derived'). A plagal mode always had the same final as its corresponding authentic mode. The authentic modal scales were notated as white-key octave scales rising from the notes *d* (mode I), *e* (mode III), *f* (mode V) and *g* (mode VII), with their corresponding plagals a fourth lower.'

"It must be remembered . . . that these notes do not stand for a specific absolute pitch . . . but were chosen simply so that the distinguishing interval patterns could be notated without the use of accidentals."

D.J. Grout, *A History of Western Music* p. 51.

3. NOTATION

The Notation: By the 13th century, the notation was placed on a four-line staff with adjoining lines and spaces each representing the interval of a second. Two Clefs representing C and F were used, and the written tones were C D E F G A B and B♭.

Lerchenlied des Bernart de Ventadorn

The Greek names were applied to the wrong modes, owing to the fact that reliable information on the early Greek system was no longer available.

Thus modes I and II came to be called Dorian and Hypodorian (meaning the Plagal version of the mode), modes III and IV became the Phrygian and Hypophyrgian modes, modes V and VI became Lydian and Hypolydian modes and modes VII and VIII became the Mixolydian and Hypomixolydian modes.

SIGHT-SINGING. In the Eleventh Century, a monk named Guido d'Arrezzo (c990–1050) developed the art of sight-singing through the use of the Hexachord and the Sol-Fa syllables. The Hexchord was a six-tone group of notes *c-d-e-f-g-a*; in which the semitone falls between the third and fourth steps and all other steps are tones.

As an aid to memorizing the pattern, the first notes of each of six phrases, in the hymn *Ut queant laxis*, began with one of the notes of the pattern and the initial syllables of these words became the names of the notes, *ut, re mi, fa, sol, la*.

This system is still used today, with a couple of minor changes; the first note has become *do* and *ti* has been added above *la*.

By transposing the Hexachord onto three notes C, G or F the system covered all the notes recognised at the time. (See page 75).

The hexachord on G used the B-Natural, for which the sign was a 'Square b' (♮) (*b quadrum*); the hexachord on F used the B-flat which used the 'round b' sign (♭), (*b rotundum*). As you can see, these signs are the forerunners of the ♮, ♯ and ♭ signs.

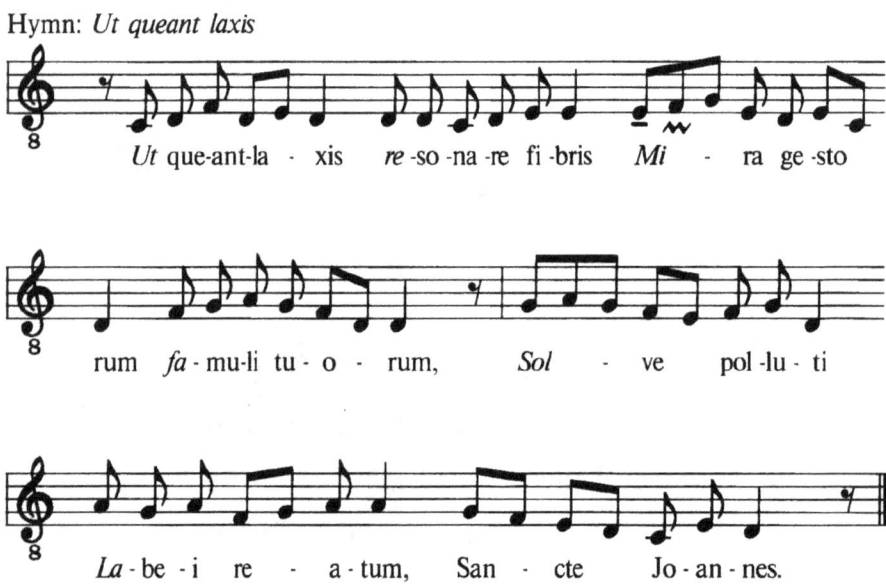

Hymn: *Ut queant laxis*

Ut que-ant-la - xis *re* -so -na -re fi -bris *Mi* - ra ge -sto

rum *fa* - mu-li tu - o - rum, *Sol* - ve pol -lu - ti

La - be - i re - a - tum, San - cte Jo - an - nes.

That thy servants may freely sing forth the wonders of thy deeds, remove all stain of guilt from their unclean lips, O Saint John.

4. MODES IN THE RENAISSANCE PERIOD

The Swiss theorist, Henricus Glareanus (also known as Glarean) (1488–1563), modified the old theory of Ecclesiastical Modes in his treatise 'Dodecachordon' (Twelve Modes or Twelve Keys). In his system, each of the six modes had an Authentic and a Plagal form, (making 12 modes). The mode on B (called Locrian by later theorists) was recognised, but dismissed as impracticable due to the interval of a Diminished 5th between the Finalis and the Dominant.

By the 1570's the Authentic and Plagal forms had merged and a system of six modes remained, with the Ionian (now our major scale) being numbered as I. Once again the names were borrowed from the Greek names (although they in no way related to them as you can see). They became as follows: I — Ionian, II — Dorian, III — Phrygian, IV — Lydian, V — Mixolydian, VI — Aeolian. With the later addition of the seventh mode, the Locrian, this is how we know the modes today.

The system of six Modes.

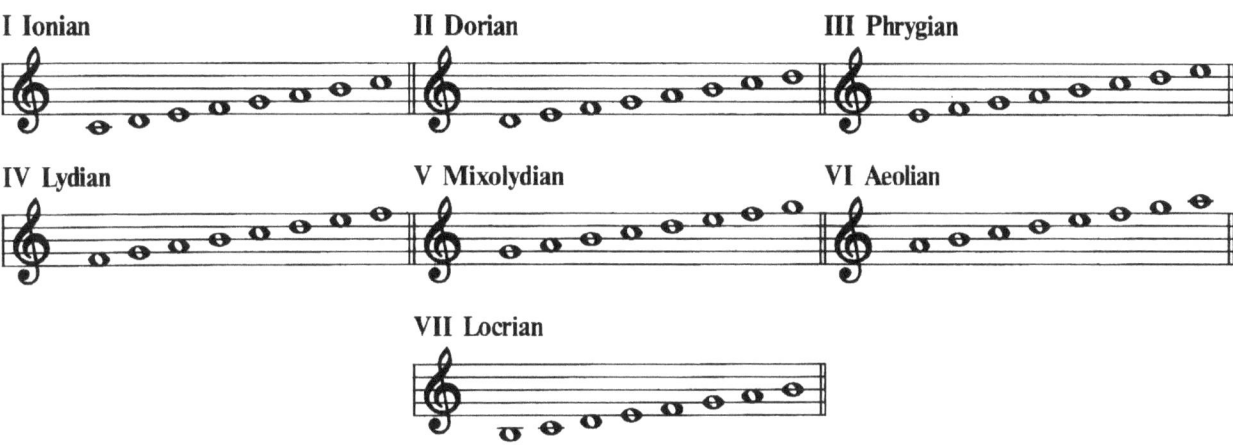

5. MUSICA FICTA

In practice, these modes were often modified by altering one of the notes. Even though a B natural was written, singers would tend to sing B♭ in many cases, as their ears would dictate the sound. This was called Musica Ficta (fictitious music).

Thus in a Lydian passage, the Augmented Fourth between the first and fourth degrees was avoided by altering the B-Natural to B-Flat. In the Mixolydian the F was raised to F-Sharp to avoid the Diminished Fifth between the third and seventh notes. As a result, both these scales sounded exactly like F and G Major respectively.

In the Dorian mode the B was often replaced by B-Flat resulting in the Natural Minor form of the scale.

Music in the Fifteenth and Sixteenth centuries has many examples of this happening, so that the move to Major and Minor scales was a gradual development over several centuries. By the Baroque period (1600–1750) the Major-Minor system largely replaced the modal system, although some vestiges of the system can still be found in the music of Bach and Handel.

The other major development in the acceptance of the Major-Minor system, was the widespread adoption of Equal-Tempered tuning, which enabled modulation to all twelve major and all twelve minor keys.

17. TELL MEE DAPHNE

TELL MEE DAPHNE is a set of variations of a popular tune which was well known to Giles Farnaby's contemporary listeners. Therefore the simple and unornamented statement of the original theme, which usually begins music in Variations form, is omitted, and the piece starts with Variation 1.

The Breve at the end of the music is redundant. As in many cases in the Fitzwilliam Virginal Book these ending Breves were an ornamental feature of the copyist's calligraphy. (The virginal was an early keyboard instrument that could be placed on a small table or on the lap. It was played mainly by young ladies, hence the name Virginal.)

The added accidentals are Musica Ficta accidentals. The F♯ and G♯ are used as they are in the Melodic Minor scale.

Play the piece at a moderate speed, so that all the contrapuntal lines can be executed properly.

Giles Farnaby (c.1565-1640)

79

5. MODERN USE OF THE MODES

After a break of 200 years or so, modern composers have begun looking at Modes as an alternate means of composition, to the Major-Minor system. There are many examples of Modes in the music of Benjamin Britten and Bela Bartok, to name two. Refer to *Contemporary Modal Pieces*, for more pieces in Modal style to study and play.

With the development of Electronic instruments such as organs and synthesisers, the old system of Just Intonation can once more be used by those composers wishing to use Modes as a basis for composition. The computerised tuning system will allow many different sounds to be stored for use by the composer so that the restrictions previously experienced, when one had to stop to retune the instrument, no longer apply.

Refer to the music of Steve Reich, Philip Glass and Terry Riley.

THE RING-TAIL POSSUM

The following piece is number nine from Contemporary Modal Pieces (Brandman). It is in the Dorian Mode beginning on G and features a melody played in Double Octave unison. Note the changing time signatures. Keep the Jazz pianist Oscar Peterson in mind when playing this piece and you will achieve the intended sound.

Dorian Mode on G

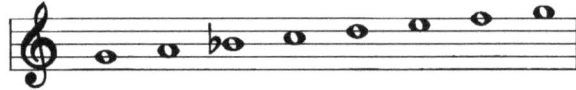

Remember that this Mode has the same pattern of black and white notes on the keyboard as F Major scale.

Refer to Pictorial Patterns for Keyboard Scales and Chords for the Modal Scales.

18. THE RING-TAIL POSSUM

IMPROVISATION AND MODES

The seven church modes discussed on page 74, when used in Jazz Improvisation, can each be seen as the parent scale of a type of four-note chord. By taking the 1st, 3rd, 5th and 7th notes from the Modes the following chords are formed:

From the Ionian — a Major 7th chord
From the Dorian — a Minor 7th chord
From the Phrygian — a Minor 7th chord
From the Lydian — Major 7th chord
From the Mixolydian — a Dominant 7th chord
From the Aeolian — a Minor 7th chord
From the Locrian — a Minor 7th Flattened 5th (Half-Diminished 7th) chord.

As you can see the two modes which suit the Major 7th chord are the Ionian and the Lydian. The three modes which suit the Minor 7th chord are the Dorian, Phrygian and Aeolian. The only mode which suits the Dominant 7th chord is the Mixolydian and the only mode which suits the Half-Diminished 7th chord is the Locrian.

Where there is a choice of mode, the scale 'colour' must be taken into consideration. For instance, the Lydian scale is a brighter sounding scale than the Ionian. The use of the Lydian scale over the Major 7th chord will therefore add brilliance to the overall sound, where as the use of the Major scale (Ionian) will produce a rather more bland effect. As a result the Lydian scale is favoured by Jazz musicians in most situations.

Similarly, the Dorian is regarded by Jazz musicians as being the best suited Mode to the Minor 7th chord. The Aeolian and Phygian scales are the darker colours for the Minor 7th. It has been said that the Aeolian scale belongs to the classical tradition while the Dorian scale belongs to the Jazz tradition.

Generally speaking therefore, when using Modes over a Jazz chord progression, the **Dorian** Mode will be used over any Minor 7th chord (and Minor 6th chord), the **Mixolydian** Mode will be used over any Dominant 7th chord, the **Locrian** will be used over any Half-Diminished 7th chord and the **Lydian** or Ionian will be used over any Major 7th (or Major 6th) chord.

Thus a distinct pattern emerges over a common chord progression such as iim7, V7, Imaj7. In C Major this chord pattern is Dm7, G7, Cmaj7. The suitable Modes would therefore be: D Dorian, G Mixolydian and C Ionian. If you compare these three modes you will notice that they are all white note scales, or looking at them another way, the same scale notes played over different ranges. If the C Lydian Mode were to be used for the last chord, a touch of G Major (that bright sound) would be introduced.

For more information on the theory and practice of Modes, refer to:
- *Contemporary Theory Workbook Book 2*
- *Contemporary Chord Workbooks 1 and 2*

For the sounds of the Modes, refer to:
- *Contemporary Aural Course, Set 7 (Hear Your Chords!)*
- *Contemporary Aural Course, Set 8 (Hear More Chords!)*

As I pointed out earlier, the Dorian scale is regarded by Jazz musicians as the best Mode for the Minor 7th chord. As a result, Jazz musicians view each Minor 7th chord as being 'Temporarily' the second chord of a key. Thus they may have many 'mini-modulations' through the course of the piece.

However, there are a few cases where the Aeolian or Phrygian Modes may be better suited. If the Minor seventh is used as chord vi of a Major key, then the Aeolian Mode would quite possibly be better suited. Similarly if the Minor 7th chord is functioning as chord iii in a Major Key the Phrygian could be better suited. Use your chord table to find out which degree is being used.

Thus in a progression which moves III, VI, II, V, I the suitable modes would be as follows: Phrygian, Aeolian, Dorian Mixolydian and Ionian. If you compare all these modes on the correct starting notes, you will find that they contain the same notes.

Complete the chord progression and provide the Modes over each chord in the manner shown. Indicate the Modes by writing in the Modal name above each bar (measure). Once completed, play the exercise.

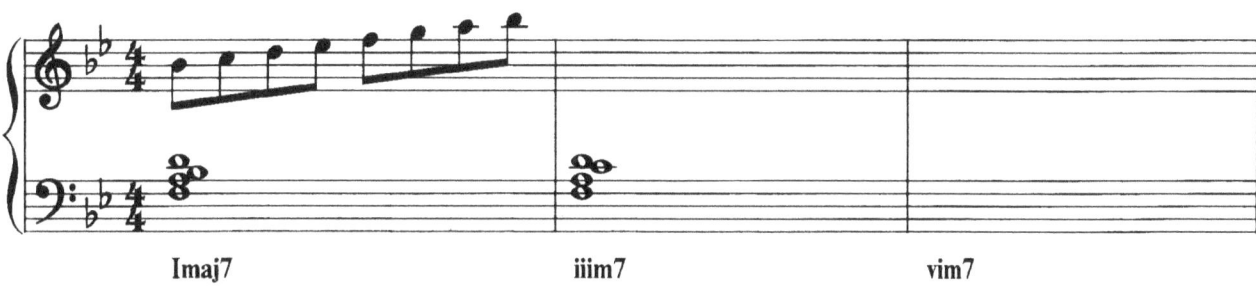

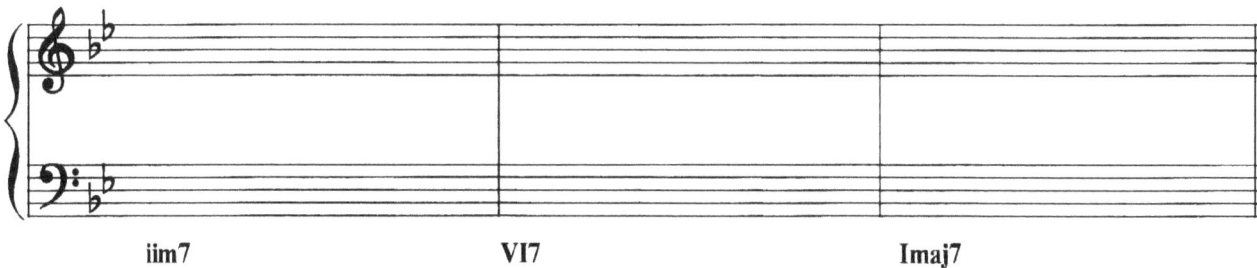

HOW TO IMPLEMENT THE MODES

In an improvised piece of music, the Left Hand usually plays the chord progression while the Right Hand plays scale, chord or sequence patterns using the notes of the particular Mode which suits the chord. Refer to the chord progressions given in this book in the section under the heading Root Progressions Step I. These progressions can be used as vehicles for improvisation using the Modes over the Left Hand chords. See pages 33 and 34.

EXTENSION NOTES

As the extension notes are added to the basic chord, as is mainly done in Jazz compositions, the choice of Mode is narrowed down in accordance with the better sounding chords.

The chart below shows the chords built from the Modal scale notes. The less frequently used chords (play them and you will hear why) are bracketed.

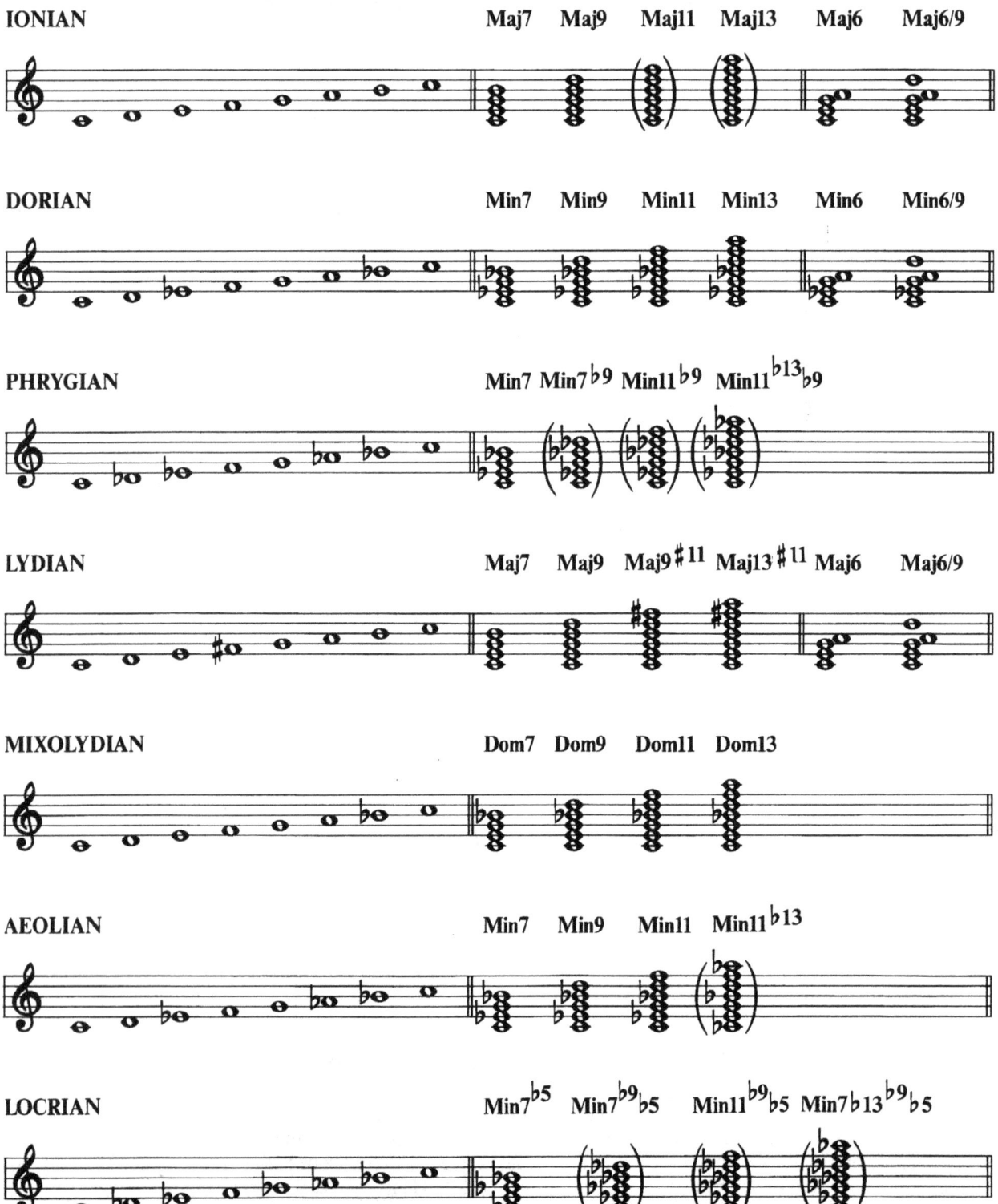

As you can see, not all types of chord are represented by the seven Modes, which is why altered scales are needed for the other chords. Refer to Book Four for some of these altered scales and the chords which they suit.

www.ingramcontent.com/pod-product-compliance
Lightning Source LLC
Chambersburg PA
CBHW081358160426
43192CB00013B/2437